Uncovering Your Church's
HIDDEN SPIRIT

CELIA ALLISON HAHN

Foreword by Tilden Edwards

The Alban Institute

Library of Congress Card Number 00-111201

ISBN 1-56699-241-9

The kingdom of heaven is like treasure hidden in a field, which someone found and hid; then in his joy he goes and sells all that he has and buys that field.

(Matt. 13:44)

CONTENTS

This pioneering book moves beyond the individual's growing concern about spirituality to explore the spiritual life of the congregation as a whole. Learnings in recent decades from the many fresh explorations of the living Spirit's guiding presence for individuals hold much promise for understanding the Spirit's guidance in the corporate life of the congregation. The process developed by Celia Hahn for turning these findings into a congregational exploration of the Spirit's presence holds further promise for developing a deeper spiritual community.

In a culture that often holds up the individual as the focus of attention, it is important to find ways to bring our awareness of God's active presence beyond the individual to the corporate circles of our lives. Individuals exist as part of a larger whole. Ultimately that wholeness is the very oneness of God, in whom we live and move and have our being. In Christian tradition wholeness is expressed with such images as the mystical Body of Christ, the holy people of God, and the belonging of all creatures to the one God. The image of God's very nature is of a oneness manifest in mutually loving, self-emptying diversity. The great spiritual art involves uniquely living out of the wholeness of God in the particulars of a time, place, and group of people. The distinctive callings of individuals are mysteriously intertwined with the callings of others, and the corporate callings of our communities, such as congregations, are fed by the range of individual callings within those bodies. We live out a dance between our individuality, community life, and the One who inspires the steps as we go along.

The congregation carries on this larger dance in its own special ways. Its story is a subplot of a larger story: the mysterious life of the Spirit and of individual and communal responses to it, threaded through Scripture and history. The backdrop of this particular story is a much larger one still:

the story of creation that shows every creature to be inextricably related to one another in a sharing of the same divine wellspring.

When we become active in a congregation, we sense something of its difference: its unique history, joys, sorrows, responses (and failed responses) to callings, and varieties of old and new people with their evolving experiences of God—all of which help to shape its ever-shifting corporate life. Within this dynamic reality of the church, certain "patterns of the Spirit" can show themselves, patterns that reveal what God seems to be up to with the church as a whole. Sensing these patterns leads to sensing the corporate callings of the congregation. This awareness can awaken a shared sense of identity and mission in the congregation.

I say "sensing" rather than "knowing" the church's callings because we are dealing with the partially hidden, mysterious, ever-dynamic life of God's Spirit in our midst, which we can never fully grasp. Celia Hahn quotes Steve Jacobsen as saying that "religion" seems dull because it is all defined and systematized, while "spirituality" is interesting because it is slippery, evocative, alive—like a deer in the forest. "We shouldn't presume to capture it or it will run away and disappear." Because of its elusiveness, though, our attempts to uncover the Spirit's life, in ourselves or in a congregation's history and current life, can be frustrating as well as exciting, and maddening to people who want a clear, defined, finished picture of reality.

I believe that congregations, like individuals, find an awesome, intimate Mystery at the heart of their being. To be in living, ongoing touch with this gracious Mystery, one needs a willingness to live while probing an expectant darkness, trusting that enough light will be given for what we need to understand and do at a given time. Though this murkiness can have a frustrating aspect, finally I think this infinite Mystery at our heart is a cause for celebration, because it means that at the center of our individual and corporate lives exists an endless potential for new life to be brought out of old. We are not confined to what we already know and do. With Paul we can rejoice that God "is able to accomplish abundantly far more than all we can ask or imagine" (Eph. 3:20). This means that we as individuals and as congregations have potentialities that are beyond our imagining, however buried these may be in our confused, willful, and oversecuring ways of seeing life. God will not give up on us, but in our freedom we can give up on God, as we miss or refuse the endless openings of the Spirit we are offered day by day.

Given this elusiveness of the Beloved, how can we proceed to discover the Spirit's movements through a congregation's life? This discovery will require an approach that respects the Spirit's subtlety and gives people a careful, prayerful, head-in-the-heart listening process that can help uncover what God wants us to hear about the church's distinctive gifts and calling, in the church's history as well as in its current life. Celia Hahn has developed a helpful process for just such an uncovering of the spirituality of a congregation, tested with five congregations and interpreted with the help of a few others who accompanied her on the sidelines throughout this action-research project. She brings together her long background in trying to understand the life of congregations with her experience in the ministry of spiritual direction, and the blend offers us a fresh possibility for approaching and understanding the congregation's soul.

Her process involves the pastor and a variety of spiritually respected people in the congregation. Flexibility is built into the steps so that the specific situations of congregations can be taken into account. In the congregations where she has tested and evolved this process, much was learned about the reality of each church's corporate spirituality. A further benefit was the power of the interviews and corporate reflection for many of the participants, revealing fresh insights and bonding people together at a deeper spiritual level. They came to a deeper awareness of how they belonged together to the mysterious but palpable life of the Spirit among them. The process also helped some people to realize how this shared spirituality feeds into their daily lives and work settings.

One fruit of Celia Hahn's work seen in this book is the value of an outside "spiritual companion" to assist a congregation as it seeks to discern the Spirit's life in its midst. Celia's current efforts to begin the development of a cadre of such companions can lead to a unique new resource for congregations, complementing the increasingly available number of people who offer one-on-one spiritual companionship. She also shows how a congregational process can be undertaken only with internal resources, if this is preferred.

My hope is that you who read this book will consider beginning such a process of identifying your congregation's corporate spirituality, and that you will share your discoveries with Celia, as she requests at the end of the book. What you can tell her from your experience will contribute to the larger knowledge that is needed to evolve further this sensitive approach to sighting the sacred deer walking in the congregation's forest.

TILDEN EDWARDS
Founder and Senior Fellow
The Shalem Institute for Spiritual Formation

A woman sitting in the pew next to me stood up and said with feeling: "I don't want just to *believe* in God; I want to *know* God." In this heart-felt exclamation during the sermon feedback time, she spoke for many people. Eighty percent of respondents to one survey said that what they most needed from their church was food for their spiritual hunger.[1] It is increasingly clear that people are bringing with them a longing for what is ultimately trustworthy as they venture through church doors today.

But as people come to you speaking of their hunger to know God, how do you find a way to be of help to them? Most seminaries have taught little or nothing about guiding people spiritually. And although spiritual guides and writers often seem to present spirituality as primarily an individual, inward enterprise, it is becoming ever clearer that people need a community if they are to grow and develop, and that not only individuals but also churches have a hidden spirit that can be uncovered. This recognition reminds me of Jesus' prayer "that they may all be one. As you, Father, are in me and I am in you, may they also be in us" (John 17:21). Loren Mead, founding president of the Alban Institute, and others emphasize that, unless churches can replace busyness and survival anxiety with a rediscovery of their spiritual center and a willingness to listen for God's call, they will continue losing energy and relevance. While mainline churches often continue to speak to those who value activist and issue-centered approaches, many seem to be losing members, while evangelical churches that stay clear about the purpose of their efforts and programs are growing. Perhaps mainliners have something to learn from evangelicals and mystics who know the importance of staying close to the center.

How can congregations effectively support people in opening themselves to that grounding in the call of the Spirit that sends them out as transformed people to a broken world? I am convinced that churches must stay close to the center, grounded in the Spirit's call, and close to the doors through which people enter bringing their longings, and through which they go out to a hungry world.

In his study of church boards, Charles Olsen found that although people volunteered to serve on boards with the hope of enhancing their spiritual growth, on completing their terms they often went away disappointed because they had experienced only a secular Robert's Rules of Order mentality.[2] I'm sure it's a lot easier for us to critique the Pharisees for their lopsided emphasis on religious busywork than to turn the same scrutiny on ourselves. But we, as church leaders today, do face the constant challenge to look *through* the "church work," the ecclesiastical concerns that make up our daily chores, to God and to the people we serve, who then go out and serve the world beyond our doors.

Staying close to the center can give us hope. In part the hope comes from not having to depend only on our own resources. I believe it also comes from keeping our eyes focused more on the gifts we have received than on the programs we have developed.

It is clear that people are experiencing a split between the spiritual search and the life of a congregation. This split has in fact existed for centuries. Monastic communities felt called to rediscover the church's spiritual purpose. However, the reforms of the religious orders seldom made their way into the parish church system. As pastoral theologian Richard Chiola put it, "Religious life was always a subversive movement that tried to compensate for the insufficiency of parish life, but ultimately supported not congregational but individual spiritual life." People inside and outside churches continue to cry out for help with their spiritual search, and we need to find ways to reunite that cry with the life of the local congregation.

BEGINNINGS OF THE RESEARCH

Having been a part of the Alban Institute's work in congregational studies for 22 years, in 1997 I began the two-year Shalem Spiritual Guidance Program. While valuing Alban's practical tools for congregations, I felt that more than "tools" were needed. And while appreciating Shalem's path to a deeper spiritual life, I frequently felt it didn't quite "touch the ground" of our corporate life in churches. I experienced a strong calling to make a beginning with a joining of congregational and spiritual strengths. I wanted to integrate the spiritual wisdom of Shalem with Alban's knowledge about congregations fed by insights from the social sciences. So I began to seek out others who were exploring the spiritual-congregational boundary and then to interview experts in spirituality and in congregations who might serve as advisors for the research. Increasingly grasped by the call to focus more deeply on those questions of congregational spirituality, I began talking to people like Chuck Olsen, author of *Transforming Church Boards*, who wrote me: "The literature of spiritual direction has not been applied in a corporate context. See the dynamics and make the translation." Bishop Ronald H. Haines, head of the Episcopal Diocese of Washington, responded to my letter announcing my plans to begin a research project on congregational spirituality: "I hear a heartfelt desire for more spiritual development all across the Diocese." The bishop invited a proposal to the Ruth Gregory Soper Memorial Trust of the diocese, which includes within its purposes "nurturing the spiritual life." As I began work on the proposal and talked to more people, I heard affirmation for this vision, this reunion of spiritual life and the life of the local church, and also hints about how to develop it further. Some important guiding principles for the research began to emerge.

I knew we must take seriously, as a foundation of the research, God-at-work in the churches. Where might we look for "the real presence" in these congregations? Richard Chiola suggested that we "look at a congregation and contemplate its life so as to know how God reveals Godself to its people," seeking the revelation that takes place by participating in God's life "not only through ideas." Tilden Edwards, founder of Shalem, said the answer to my question lay in prayer—"asking the Spirit to show you what you need to understand." Such conversations clarified my conviction that we must take seriously God's presence in the gathered body, and have faith that we would come to know God-at-work in this study.

I knew that we must use research tools, but also take on faith the divine Presence, not remain simply enclosed within the sociology of religion. Steve Jacobsen, who had recently finished a study reported in his book *Hearts to God, Hands to Work: Connecting Spirituality and Work*,[3] shared with me his insights about the connection between research and spirituality:

The sociological model tends to prefer objectivity and whatever is quantifiable, but spirituality is clearly more elusive than that. It became clear to me that the reason why "spirituality" has become so popular is that it currently is denoting, at least in part, subjective reality and experience. "Religion" seems dull because it is all defined and systematized. "Spirituality" is interesting because it is slippery, personal, evocative, alive . . . like a deer in the forest. We shouldn't presume to capture it or it will run away and disappear.

Yes! For me, "spiritual" means anything that speaks about that restlessness of our hearts, our yearning for or sense of connection with God, and, in this project, about that connection as we know it within the communion of our parish life. Like Steve, I wanted to uncover this alive, evocative, immediately present yet slippery, hidden spiritual life.

GATHERING ADVISORS, MAPPING THE STUDY

Through these conversations, I gathered a broadly ecumenical research advisory committee for the Congregational Spirituality Project, including two consultants:

- Tilden Edwards, executive director of the Shalem Institute for Spiritual Formation
- Gerald G. May, M.D., Shalem's director for research and program development

The research advisory committee members, each of whom served as special consultant to one church in the study, were:

- Corinne Ware of the Episcopal Seminary of the Southwest, Austin, Texas, author of *Discover Your Spiritual Type*
- Charles M. Olsen, director of Worshipful Work, author of *Transforming Church Boards*
- John Ackerman, author of *Spiritual Awakening*
- Richard Chiola, a Roman Catholic priest who has taught pastoral theology at Yale Divinity School and at St. John's University, Collegeville, Minnesota
- Robert K. Martin, then professor of pastoral and practical theologies and Christian Education at Yale Divinity School

Participating Alban Institute Staff members included:

- Ian Evison, director of research
- James P. Wind, president

Advisors included members of the following denominations: Presbyterian, Episcopal, United Methodist, Roman Catholic, Evangelical Lutheran, and Unitarian Universalist.

As we moved toward interviews with people in the parishes, I paused to ponder further with the research advisory committee and a group of other interested thinkers: "What major convictions must guide this research project?"

We were clear that God is at work in the churches. In addition to using social-scientific tools, this research needed to take that truth seriously. John Ackerman put it this way: "It seems to me that you are trying to involve the congregations in discerning the real presence of Christ." Robert Martin suggested, "Ask: 'What are these people allowing God to do with them?'"

What did that major conviction say about how I should engage in the research, as project director? I was clear that:

- I needed to walk in "open to what is" in the churches, and to pray for the grace to move into them in a spiritual companionship mode: present to God and present in the moment with the people. Chuck Olsen added that an important way to be in the research was to "listen to the movements of the Spirit. The study will take on a life of its own."
- I needed to listen to people respectfully and attentively.
- The study needed to be an empowering inquiry, avoiding the sometimes disempowering effect of working with a supposed "expert."

BEGINNING WORK WITH THE CHURCHES

With the preliminary spadework well underway, the project funded by the Soper Trust, and the parishes chosen on the basis of their interest and diversity representative of the Episcopal Diocese of Washington, we went to work on the first year's tasks, designed to surface the churches' gifts and to learn as much as possible about the churches' corporate spirituality. To accomplish those tasks, I visited the churches and interviewed the five parishioners identified as "sages" by their peers and the rector (pastor) of each of five congregations.[4] In the second year, I returned to the churches and, with the rector (and, in one church, lay leaders, too), designed and carried out discernment meetings. The meetings began with a presentation of the congregation's gifts I had seen through the interviews and offered an opportunity for interviewees to enhance or correct that description. We then moved into discernment: Given these gifts, what is God calling us to be, and perhaps do, now? At the end of each year's work, the research advisory committee met at the Alban Institute, and we talked about what I had been learning. The findings thus became collaborative, enriched by many perspectives. Later in the book we will listen in on a few of those illuminating discussions.

We selected five very different project churches. (We had hoped for six, but regrettably a primarily African-American congregation had to withdraw because of a sudden clergy vacancy, which would claim the church's energies and deprive it of consistent clergy leadership during the project.) The five are:

- Ascension, Silver Spring (a Maryland suburb close to, and merging into, Washington, D.C.)
- St. Thomas' Parish, Dupont Circle (in Northwest Washington)
- St. Peter's, Poolesville (an hour's drive from the city, in the Maryland countryside)
- St. Patrick's, in the Foxhall area of Northwest Washington (next to Georgetown)
- Ascension, Lexington Park (a two-hour drive into Southern Maryland)

The five participating parishes represented much of the diversity of the diocese. Although the project was funded by this Episcopal diocese, and although the research experts were united in their conviction that it would make no sense for a study of this size to include several denominations, I always saw the need to do this study in such a way that the findings would communicate clearly across denominational lines (a task that seemed much easier in a study on spirituality than in matters related more closely to denominational polity).

How This Book Is Organized

This book is based on the stories of the five congregations. Each illuminates different parts of the puzzle of congregational spirituality, so the stories of various congregations are told in separate chapters. Some of these churches will teach theoretical lessons about congregational spirituality; others will shed light on practical ways to proceed. Some are generalists; others have particular areas of expertise.

In part 1, "What Is Congregational Spirituality?" we'll probe for answers by listening to the stories of the churches whose lives seem to speak especially to that question: Ascension (Silver Spring) and St. Thomas' Parish. Before each church steps up to our lectern, I'll ask you to join me in a Sunday morning visit and a look at its history. We'll also meet St. Peter's, Poolesville, one of whose important lessons is about "being the church in this place." Since I assume many readers are exploring congregational spirituality for the sake of uncovering their own church's hidden spirit, I invite you to pause from time to time to reflect prayerfully on how those stories connect with your church's stories. If you are reading this book as a small group, you might begin your gatherings with these meditations.

Although this is intended to be a practical book, it's not going to *feel* particularly practical in part 1 (unless you *make* it practical through the reflections just described). I learned early that I had to sound like a broken record with the project churches: "Discern first; plan later." That approach will also shape the structure of the book. We can't plan our route until we know the direction in which we are called to go, and we can't move forward without some light on the path immediately ahead. And that's why, as we explore part 1, "What is Congregational Spirituality?," I will invite you from time to time to intersperse your reading with prayerful consideration of your church's spirituality, alone or with a group of interested church members. These reflections are an integral part of the process.

In part 2, "Discernment: Who Are We Called to Be? Where Are We Called to Go?" we'll find we have much to learn from three churches that were especially eager to give themselves to the discernment process—St. Patrick's Church, the Church of the Ascension in Lexington Park, and St. Peter's. Again, we will introduce the churches through a Sunday morning visit, ponder their stories a bit, and then join them in a discernment meeting. As we proceed through part 2 and move on to part 3—the most practical part of the book, "Uncovering Your Church's Hidden Spirit"—the five churches, now old friends, will return to teach us further lessons, as we consider our own congregation's possible path to spiritual deepening.

PART I

What Is Congregational Spirituality?

As you have sent me into the world, so I have sent them. . . . I ask not only on behalf of these, but also on behalf of those who will believe in me through their word, that they may all be one. As you, Father, are in me and I am in you, may they also be in us, so that the world may believe that you have sent me.

(John 17:18, 20-21)

All One Body We

A s we journey through the churches' stories, we will uncover several links between the words "congregational" and "spirituality." Congregations do have a discernible spiritual identity, we will learn as we listen to the people of these churches and try to see the congregation's spirit and gifts through their eyes. Your church's spirit is not unlike yours: the core of who you are—where you really live, where your heart is, your history with God and an identity known to God, who keeps calling you back as well as calling you out to the work you've been given to do. In Revelation this corporate spirit is addressed as the "Angel" of the church, who says at the end of the message to each church, "Those who have ears to hear, *let them hear*" (italics added), which is the task of discernment. The Orthodox would see this Angel as the bishop. (The churches in the project had an empty chair for the bishop at the front of the church, and I like the idea of seeing that empty chair as symbolizing also, beyond the bishop, that church's Angel.)

As we describe our attempt to come to know the Angels, the hidden spirits of the project churches, a few words on how we began the process may help set the stage. The members of the congregation chose the interviewees, and I provided each interviewee ahead of time with a simple set of questions from *Discover Your Spiritual Type*, by Corinne Ware.[1] (I will introduce this questionnaire briefly here, and discuss it in more detail, along with a process for identifying the interviewees, in part III.) The questionnaire gives people a way to name and understand their spiritual experience as individuals and as a congregation. Do they experience God primarily in a speculative (intellectual) or affective (heartfelt) way? Is their spirituality apophatic (sensing God as mystery) or kataphatic (knowing God as revealed, in words and images)? One's answers to these questions point to one or more types for the individual and his or her congregation:

The Spirituality Wheel_©
A Selector for Spiritual Type

Corinne D. Ware, D. Min.

Based on a spirituality typology developed by Urban T. Holmes

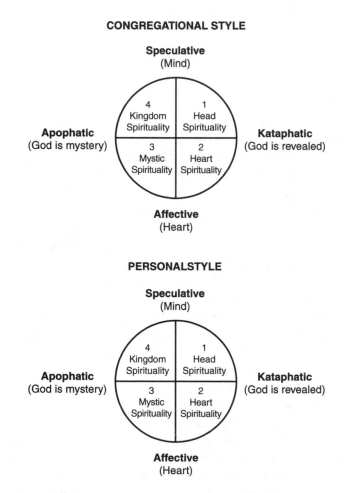

Adapted from *The History of Christian Spirituality: An Analytical Introduction* by Urban T. Homes, © The Seabury Press. Used by Permission of Jane Holmes, Executrix.

Look at the circle diagram with two intersecting lines. Note to readers: The vertical line indicates *how we go about knowing*. Some of us tend to go about knowing more through our rational minds—with our heads. Others of us go about knowing with our hearts, our feelings. The horizontal line indicates *how we conceptualize God*. Some of us conceptualize God in an emptying ("apophatic") way. We know God as mystery. This is a more receptive way. Others conceptualize God in an imaging ("kataphatic") way. In this more active way, we see God as revealed, knowable. We need both active and receptive ways, and we can develop both ways. Spiritual wholeness means including all parts of the circle, even if that means just appreciating the others.

The *four quadrants* identify four types of spirituality: quadrant 1, Head Spirituality; quadrant 2, Heart Spirituality; quadrant 3, Mystic Spirituality; quadrant 4, Kingdom Spirituality. For more guidance on the use of the Ware instrument, see chapter 11.

Since this is not a forced-choice questionnaire, it gives people room to look at the wholeness of their experience as individuals and as people in community seeking to love God with heart, soul, mind, and strength. The experience of taking the test indicates that

- As individuals and congregations, we are stronger in some ways of experiencing God than others
- We need one another as complementary members of the body of Christ
- Everybody is included in the spiritual quest (including "head" spirituality types, who often have not seen themselves—or been seen—as "spiritual")

Interviewees answered a simple set of questions—first from their own point of view, second as they thought most people in their congregation would answer. The instrument provided a helpful "diving board" into the interview, introducing some common language.

The use of the questionnaire helped us begin talking about some important realities that we sometimes forget. First, spirituality exists deep inside each person and also in the person's world—and here we are looking particularly at congregations. On each level, speaking about spirituality means talking about the whole.

Looking within, we see that spirituality is about a *whole person*. Mordechai Liebling, executive director of the Jewish Reconstructionist Federation, speaks about that wholeness when he describes the yearnings of today's searchers to be fully engaged—yearnings that they bring when they walk through the door of a house of worship: "We live on four levels— physical, emotional, intellectual and spiritual," said Liebling. "In order for religion to work, it has to address people on all four levels."[2]

But we speak here of a *community* of people seeking spiritual life together. Henri Nouwen, Dutch-born priest and writer on spirituality, describes the organic nature of the person-community bond: "Just because prayer is so personal and arises from the center of our life, it is to be shared with others. Just because prayer is the most precious expression of being human, it needs the constant support and protection of the community to grow and flower. . . . [P]rayer . . . should always remain embedded in the life of the community of which we are part. . . . [W]e do not have to wait alone."[3]

Looking around us, we can see that not only is every person uniquely engaged in a life journey, but so is every congregation. In a great many Alban research projects, it has been demonstrated that churches are as different from each other as people are. In this study, the uniqueness of each congregation, its distinctness from every other church, was again made abundantly clear—this time in regard to its spiritual life.

Carrying with us the idea that spirituality also concerns the whole person's search for a whole way of being in the world, a search carried out in the body of the congregation, let us look for congregations' spirituality in stories of their lives—their struggles, their worship, their ways of "becoming one" despite differences that commonly separate people, and their call to show forth their spirituality in the world.

CHAPTER 1

Strong at the Broken Places

When through the deep waters I call thee to go,
The rivers of woe shall not thee overflow;
For I will be with thee, thy troubles to bless
And sanctify to thee thy deepest distress.[1]

A church living out of the power of its corporate spiritual identity may find itself strong at the broken places—places where suffering is revealed as "the outer clothing of growth."[2] Let us now explore journeys "through deep waters" at the Church of the Ascension in Silver Spring, and at St. Thomas' Parish.

EXODUS AND NEW LIFE

The Church of the Ascension discovered new life after the exodus of a large number of parishioners.

When I first visited the Rev. Mary Sulerud, the rector (senior pastor), and Jennifer Woods, the senior warden (chief lay officer of the vestry, or church board), I had a sense of a neighborhood parish that is eager to get past the common church program focus. Mary stressed the parish's energized commitment to respond to the busy and harried quality of people's lives—to focus on offering them nourishment for their daily lives in the world rather than giving them more things to do that leave them wearier. (Ascension resists sponsoring activities on Saturdays, for example.)

Join me on my next visit—on Pentecost. The congregation was a mix of people of different races and ages, many wearing red in honor of the festival day. The diversity of this church seemed to be an important source of energy. Pentecost is an important feast day for Ascension Church, and the service provided me with a sense of the vitality of this rector and the congregation.

The same vigor that I sensed in Mary when I first visited her was palpable as she led this service. In her sermon she said, "The Spirit gives us the possibility of crossing all the boundaries" that separate people. It "makes friends of strangers." Another comment of Mary's emphasized the energy I'd already observed: "This day breathes on us the fiery reality" that we are not just another human service organization. "Fiery reality" felt like a good fit with the vibrancy of this place.

People dressed comfortably for the heat of the unair-conditioned church. (Plans for installing an air-conditioning system, along with other improvements to the plant, were presented by an architect after the service.)

The rather high-church service (including genuflecting, portions of the service sung, a procession of the Gospel) was energized, not stiff. The liturgy seemed a receptive ground for nurturing the many richnesses in this congregation. The service held together diverse elements. Both *The Hymnal 1982* (Episcopal) and *Lift Every Voice and Sing II*, an African-American hymnal produced by the Episcopal Church[3] were found in the pews. The guitar group at communion further enriched my impression of liveliness, and "something for everyone"—letting the music bring together people from different traditions.

A congregation that reflects the enormous variety (racial and every other kind) blooming in a close-in suburb-becoming-city, Ascension was born as a children's choir in 1920, when the rector of nearby Grace Church felt there was a need for a church within Silver Spring proper. With approval of the bishop of Washington, Holy Innocents Mission met, including "people of all faiths"—that is, denominations. In 1929 a frame structure was built, and members of the mission chose the name Ascension. An English village neo-Gothic church and a rectory were built in the '30s and '40s. Now a congregation of 450 members ("members" meaning "baptized, attending three times a year, and in the parish register," clarifies the rector), the church has as its mission statement: "The Church of the Ascension . . . is a multiracial and socially diverse community of Anglican Christians, a part of the Family of God, who share the Church's mission to restore all people in unity with God and each other in Christ."

Ascension has been through some rough times and transitions in the past couple of decades. When the previous rector opened up a leadership lock, people who had headed the same committees for up to 20 years had to turn over their posts. About 30 of them left the parish. During their tenure Silver Spring had become an even more diverse community: now, suddenly, the great variety of people in this changing community was represented in leadership positions across the parish.

Interviewees looked back at this painful exodus, when core leaders left the parish, leaving it shaken, and they realize that the church has become strong at that broken place. Two parish leaders told the story.

Woody and I discussed the 15 or 20 years when the same people ran things at Ascension:

WOODY: If there was any criticism that you had about a specific activity, people would personalize that. Saying "Maybe we should do the straw-berry festival a little earlier next year" would ruffle the feathers of the leaders. . . . So that was the battle cry of the Grand Exodus: "We've Always Done It This Way!" The energy from diversity . . . was born out of the Grand Exodus.

CELIA: So do you think that Emmett [rector at that time] disenfranchised these leaders from a sense that this was their rightful domain for the purpose of creating more fluidity and openness in the church?

WOODY: I would say yes. But I think there's a certain amount of truth in that, and I think there's a certain amount of God-intervention.

CELIA: You are really painting a clear picture of a theme that runs through the life of this congregation, having to do with openness and inclusiveness and a readiness for change.

WOODY: That is very clearly how I see the church.

CONNIE: But when that happened [after people left], you know, I think there's always good that can come out even from the bad situation. And it gave people who perhaps had not thought in terms of leadership roles the opportunity. . . . And not only the leadership, but it opened up par-ticipation, in the choir, for instance. . . . I think it's one of the exciting things I find in the church. . . . I think it has added to the beauty of life.

Describing her leadership vision, Mary Sulerud noted that when she came to Ascension, "First we had to get over the exhaustion [from the hard times that the church had just experienced], and second we had to be reminded of who we were. . . . [They needed to hear:] 'You are loved, you need to be reminded of who you are, we are all beggars at the table first.'"

The new rector saw the task as showing forth the holiness of the people's lives. "It's almost as though we're at the Eucharist and the window is thrown open to heaven, and there is all that holiness that stands up one side of that window and there is all that holiness that is potential and real and broken on the other, and my job is to keep working with myself and others, and to keep yoked together, so that one day those images are the same. . . . The people and I are yoked on the same plow team."

Practical theologian Robert Martin, the advisory committee member who gave special attention to Ascension, summed up Mary's leadership: "She assumes more is going on than she knows. She is showing people we don't go out in the world and do things until we understand ourselves as people who are first beggars at the table of the Lord. That's key to her ministry as the icon Christ reflecting back to them their own Christlikeness."

Ascension's story indicates that diversity, when allowed to come into its own vibrance within a congregation, by the removal of a "lock" on the leadership, can result in a "plow team" of all the members, yoked in unity through the Eucharist, in which God is seen as more utterly "other" (holy) than any individual member is from another.

I invite you to stop here for a few minutes.

Take a deep breath, right down to your middle.

As you breathe out, let all tension flow out.

Sitting aware on the edge of mystery,
With God as your companion,
sense the heart of your church.

Prayerfully consider the following questions:

Is there any sense that you and your fellow members
of your church community are "yoked together on the
same plow team"?

Do you recall any dreams (or thoughts upon waking)
about your church that seem to invite prayerful
attention?

RISING FROM THE RUINS

Now let's look at this theme of strength at the broken places in another church. Come and join me in a visit to St. Thomas' Parish, on Dupont Circle, where a fire, probably set by an arsonist, destroyed the church building. In and among the ruins of the burned church a carefully tended park now welcomes the neighborhood. Worship takes place in a multipurpose room, a large, plain rectangle; 150 of the 220 members attend each Sunday.

On the Sunday morning of my visit, early arrivals were middle-aged, but of the people who came in late, large numbers were young men, often in pairs, along with a few young women. The rector, the Rev. Jim Holmes, preached a "teaching" sermon, in which the theme was "There are no outsiders." At the end of the service the rector departed in procession, and the congregation remained seated, listened to the postlude music, and applauded at the end. The liturgy may be formal, but people's way of interacting and of greeting me was certainly not formal. At the coffee hour I had a sense of a most friendly church. I talked to bright people who let me know they appreciated the intellectual challenge of St. Thomas'. One gay man said he hoped the church wouldn't become totally gay, because he treasured the variety of people, and liked seeing babies and young families in the congregation.

Let's pause for a few key notes from the church's story. From its beginning in 1891, St. Thomas's history was full of signs of success, including the presence of Franklin D. Roosevelt on the vestry. (He later attended the 11 A.M. service the day after his inauguration.) A long period of support only from pew rentals (and control by the renters) ended with the institution of an every-member canvass in 1948. The organ installed in the 1960s was considered one of the most beautiful in Washington, and music still plays a central role in St. Thomas's life and worship. Early one morning in 1970, the church burned to the ground, the blaze started apparently with gasoline by unknown arsonists. Four years later the choirmaster of St. Thomas' was found stabbed at his nearby apartment. He died of his wounds.

Interviewees filled in the story of what happened after the fire destroyed St. Thomas's church building:

HAL: As far as cliques and in-church politics, we've been blessed ever since the fire burned that out. . . . Before the fire . . . it was a very conservative, prestigious church. . . . The first Sunday after the fire, while it was still smelling of smoke out there, Henry Breul [then rector] wore the gaudiest, most colorful chasuble you've ever seen in your life, and conducted a Eucharist in the parking lot out there that was just absolutely mind-boggling in its impact. And there was not room for defeatism or anything else. . . . The people who stayed, stayed for reasons other than buildings and prestige and social status, because there was no building, there was no prestige, and there was no social status. . . . [The] Phoenix Rising committee [conducted] focus groups . . . to determine . . . what should St. Thomas' be. . . . People decided that "No, we don't want to put our resources into a building. We want to maintain our presence here. We'll make a park [out of the burned sanctuary]." . . . It was a revelation for me to see how a bunch of committed Christians can create an absolutely gangbusters [place to]worship . . . out of some ruins. . . . The buildings aren't all that important . . .—it's the worship and the spirit. . . . The fire was a tragedy in many ways; it was a blessing in others. . . . The fire cleansed us in a way: the residual people were . . . unusually committed to some basic things. . . . So those things—the space, the commitment of the people, the leadership—came together and began to build something that was unique. And that's why I think that the fire in many ways was God's will.

E.C.: The fire was a traumatic and horrible thing . . . there had to be the leadership of God to . . . pull together and make something new out of that. Because it was not the same parish at all after the fire as before the fire.

A parishioner who had come to St. Thomas' Parish well after these dramatic events summarized this "phoenix rising" period as members' "rebirth experience from the fire . . . a holy event to them—a resurrection."

Take a deep breath, right down to your middle.

As you breathe out, let all tension flow out.

Sitting aware on the edge of mystery,
Envision a burnt-out forest making room for the begin-
nings of new growth.

With God as your companion, consider Hal's words:
"The fire was a tragedy in many ways;
It was a blessing in others."

Have you and your church ever lost something and
then found something that, in retrospect, seemed very
precious?

Let your mind go back over a painful place in your
own church's life.

Has any strength been given to you through this time?

Is more healing needed?

Through Deep Waters

In individual spiritual development, we know that often it is times of "desolation," events experienced as unpleasant occasions, when things appeared to be falling apart, that prove to be vehicles for grace and growth in people's lives. As one spiritual guide puts it, "In our experiences of powerlessness . . . we come to realize that new life is given. . . . Faith is the readiness to enter into this long process of the destruction . . . of our false images of God, in order to allow God to be God."[4]

And we know from stories in the Hebrew Scriptures that the people of God long ago learned to attend to these holy sequences of bondage and liberation, desolation and grace. The blessings that may follow a sojourn "through deep waters" are also held up powerfully in the New Testament:

[A]nyone who loses his life . . . will find it. (Matt. 16:25)

It was fitting that God . . . should make the pioneer of their salvation perfect through sufferings." (Heb. 2:10)

But because we have not generally brought that perspective on tough times to the lives of churches, we may be depriving ourselves of a primary source of hope. The questions that might give birth to that hope are often not asked.

Let's look at two levels of questions that might be asked about a struggling congregation. If you ask, "How is God leading this church?" or "Where might this painful experience be leading us?" the answers are different from those voiced when you put a "human-sciences template" over the church fight or fire, and approach the story with the question: "What steps can we take to resolve this?" Conflict management is, of course, helpful. Asking "How do we resolve this problem?" produces useful answers in the "expertise" column. But when churches ask questions only on a "how to," "efficiency" level, they may assume that they're to be successful by their own efforts alone. The question about God's leading goes deeper, evoking stories that make us aware we are discerning our holy history. *Both* levels of questioning are important, and I hope that they can be joined in the same process. Just imagine what it might mean if more congregations could live their way through the hard chapters of their corporate life with a faith that God is leading them to a new land. And imagine that they had also established practices like telling the story of that hard passage as habits that would carry them along the ongoing journey.

For Ascension and St. Thomas' Parish, it was as though a rock crashed into the stream of congregational life, and then the stream found a way to flow on to a new future. Churches like these, "understanding their lives in the pattern of the Paschal mystery" (as Tilden Edwards put it), can give the rest of us hope and trust: We can say, "With all the pain, let's look forward to whatever path the river takes around the rock." These churches are in labor: "[Y]ou will have pain, but your pain will turn into joy. When a woman is in labor, she has pain, because her hour has come. But when her child is born, she no longer remembers the anguish because of the joy" (John 16:20b-22).

"TELLING OUR STORY"—A CRUCIAL "LITURGY"

Looking at these stories of congregations that live in the existential aware-ness of how their story meets the Story, we need to attend not only to the content of the event but also to the way congregations live with their story as a holy story. Jim Holmes, rector of St. Thomas', gets old-timers to retell the fire story periodically—just as stories like the Exodus had to be told and retold. They "love to tell the story." Jim says: "The fire hasn't really stopped." In some important way the people of St. Thomas' still live in the spirit of this fire-event.

Telling the story has also been one of Ascension's gifts throughout its history. One form it has taken is a gift which advisor Robert Martin called "the vigorous and impolitic naming of hidden truths which have the possibil-ity of strangling the congregation." Now many years after Ascension's "exodus," Mary Sulerud says, "We have a new story." The project inter-views "allowed us to revisit controversy and conflict with a very different sense of God's presence." As the story is reinterpreted and becomes even clearer, she emphasizes the need to be "intentional about telling the new story." So story, seen as holy story, is not static, but a living, ongoing, and life-giving reality.

Pause here for a bit. Look over your church's written history, if you have one—perhaps a brief version.

Take a deep breath, right down to your middle.

As you breathe out, let all tension flow out.

Sitting aware on the edge of mystery,
Read over your parish history, stopping when it seems right.

At what points did or do you experience God as your companion? What is your holy story?

CHAPTER 2

Listening through the Liturgy

*Because there is one bread, we who are many are one body,
for we all partake of the one bread.*

(1 Cor. 10:17)

A s we reviewed the parish data, I occasionally asked the research advisory committee: "Does this church's life seem organically *rooted* in the liturgy or is it just 'something we do'?" The stories of some of these churches provide a picture of how liturgy can be a foundation and expression of corporate spirituality.

At St. Thomas' I talked with one woman brought up a Southern Baptist, who spoke about her experience of language in churches. The language here "lends itself to meditation," she said. And, from worshiping there, I also sense that behind the liturgical words of St. Thomas' there's a lot going on. People seem to listen not only *to* but *through* these words.

JIM HOLMES: I think I have never been in a congregation where worship was as consciously central to the life of the parish as it is here. . . . I find, for me, as a cleric, the worship life here much more nourishing than I've found it in other places. I think it's really hard for clergy to be nourished in their own parish on Sunday morning. So that's one of the things that has enriched me spiritually.

CELIA: You are making me wonder whether it isn't more possible for you to be nurtured by a Sunday morning service that's very liturgically focused rather than depending a lot on what you drum up and present that's all fresh.

JIM: Yes.

CELIA: Because, in a sense, liturgy carries it.

JIM: The liturgy carries it, and I find a liturgy that is—I think somebody used the word "transparent" in the interviews, and that's a word I used when I came and interviewed with the search committee. I want everybody who is there to know what's going on. . . . We are not here doing our own stuff. We are really quite faithful to the [prayer]book. I feel good about that. And that gives me some real freedom in worship as well not to be needing to explain what is going on.

The word "transparent" was used by interviewees to describe the liturgy at St. Thomas'. People could look *through* the words and symbols to the divine. The transparency is also related to the space. Jim said, "I think the building helps with that [the transparency] as well, because it's all right out front." Another interviewee added: "Nothing gets in the way of the altar." In this liturgy, held in a simple multipurpose room, "a room you can't hide in, . . . people have to encounter each other," Jim said. People are *involved* in the liturgy."

"We look at each other," a member added. "Our eyes are not pulled toward the walls" (as they would have been in the original church building). Nor are they focused primarily on the preacher.

Mystery leaves room for doubt, people told me. (Remember this church's namesake, doubting Thomas.) "What we believe" does not hold a central place. People at St. Thomas' are opposed to anyone's pushing an opinion on someone else. People are not here to be "fixed." The other person is holy ground, and deserves respect. (How important respect must be in a gay-straight community!)

The rootedness of spirituality in the *being* of the congregation (not only the "doing") opens itself to embracing many styles of spirituality. "We do it this way here" may not. As the body of Christ, we can be more whole precisely by cherishing the differences. The centrality of worship connects not only the differences among us but also our conscious and unconscious selves.

The transparency of liturgy seems to provide spiritual room for mystics. At least three of the interviewees surfaced in this congregation were Quadrant 3 mystics on the Ware instrument—heart-centered spiritual people who see God as mystery (see diagram on page 4). This is not a Quadrant 3 parish; it is, however, respectful and open to mystics.

So St. Thomas' spirituality shines through the transparent liturgy. The liturgy's transparency is related to mystery. You see *through* the liturgy and enter into it and may be transformed.

Roman Catholic spiritual writer Thomas Merton helps clarify the transparent quality of the liturgy when he speaks of the "transcendent physical presence" that "characterizes the eucharist." He explains:

The bonds that unite us with those we love are invisible bonds. . . . The presence of friends to one another is very real . . . palpably physical . . . and yet invisible. Contemplative life is a human response to the fundamental fact that the central things in life, although spiritually perceptible, remain invisible in large measure and can very easily be overlooked by the inattentive, busy, distracted person that each of us can so readily become. The contemplative looks not so much around things but through them into their center.[1]

People at St. Thomas' look through the liturgy to the center.

Ascension, too, is more focused on liturgy than on preaching. As advisor Richard Chiola commented, "This church is held together by the liturgy." The liturgy is celebrational, giving the visitor a sense that this church is more incarnational in its way of being church—less head-oriented, less "a word place"—than many sermon-centered churches would be. Remember Mary's central vision:

It's almost as though we're at the Eucharist and the window is thrown open to heaven, and there is all that holiness that stands up one side of that window and there is all that holiness that is potential and real and broken on the other, and my job is to keep working with myself and others, and to keep yoked together, so that one day those images are the same.

Several interviewees in both these churches told me, in one way or another, that they listen *through* the liturgy. Maybe this "listening-through" has some elements in common with other practices—praying the rosary, or singing hymns from the heart—a reaching for something different from one-dimensional newspaper-front-page truth. As sociologist Robert Wuthnow[2] has posited, we may have moved from a time of dwelling in a stable spiritual home, through a period of open (and often disconnected) individual searching, to a time when a spirituality of *practice* might embrace both spiritual journeying and wisdom from the tradition. Dorothy Bass says, "[P]ractices . . . are not abstract obligations, rules, or ideas; rather they are patterns of living that are full of meaning."[3] And today's journey-ers are increasingly discovering meaning in practices.

I sense that people at St. Thomas' and Ascension move into a myste-rious contemplative presence through the liturgy. Perhaps this is one reason why liturgy seems to be moving toward a more central place in many de-nominations. Recently I talked with a conservative Baptist pastor who de-scribed the liturgical elements increasingly finding an important place in his church's worship. This liturgical way is different from a creedal approach. "Is this belief correct?" That question reaches for something important, but it may put us into an argumentative frame of mind that is different from the path toward encountering a mystery. We cannot grasp mystery head-on. The traditional, typical evangelical, free-church approach—leaving liturgy aside and trying to grasp the-truth-for-now in fresh words—is also different from looking through the liturgy, and offers both promise and cost. The freely chosen words are often arrestingly contemporary, but to take in this engaging new message we have to stare right *at* the words—which may make it harder to look *through* them, and the shimmer of mystery may fade.

The multivalence that liturgy offers is, in my view, further enhanced when worship planners intentionally include our lives in the worship. Our corporate and individual lives may be gathered into the service

- In the prayers of the people ("I lost my job—pray for me")
- Through stories in sermons (like one preached in my own parish, which ended, "He found his resentments became rusty swords in his closet—wounding only him")
- In sermon-planning task forces in which the counterpoint of life, liturgy, and lectionary can be lifted out of the daily experiences of laity and woven into stories for the preacher to offer back to the people
- In a sermon seminar where people can talk back to the preacher—witnessing to moments of truth that came to them as they listened out of their lives

This dance between life and ancient words may yield moments of trans-forming encounter between life and word. And, gathered in one body, we can share our journey of transformation as we walk amid life's challenges and Sunday's familiar words, which bridge the gap between mystery and revelation.

Take a deep breath, right down to your middle.

As you breathe out, let all tension flow out.

Sitting aware on the edge of mystery,
With God as your companion, imagine settling down in
a pew of your church as a worshiper.

Amid all the richness of the service, do you find places
where silence or music invite the worshiper's own
prayerful pondering?

Do you encounter moments when you can take in the
words and try them on?

Do you meet familiar words that may become transpar-
ent for you?

(If it is too hard to get out of role in your own church,
try visiting another church where you can anonymously
relax and pray.)

CHAPTER 3

Diversity and Social Change as "Being"

[T]he new self . . . is being renewed . . . according to the image of its creator. In that renewal there is no longer Greek and Jew, circumcised and uncircumcised . . . . slave and free, but Christ is all and in all.

(Col. 3:10-11)

Long-term member Connie knows the long story of how Ascension Church, Silver Spring, became diverse from decades ago to the present. She remembers "when Annie Wilson came to church—I took her and her children to church and back home. She was the Rosa Parks of Ascension. . . . And I just feel that everybody should have an opportunity to work out their own role within a parish, regardless of background or color or anything else. Or what church denomination you come from."

DIVERSITY AS A CORPORATE SPIRITUAL GIFT

I asked: "So it sounds as though the church's becoming more varied, with more kinds of people from the community attending the church, is a really important movement at this time?"

CONNIE: I think it is. I think it's one of the exciting things I find in the church . . . . I think it has added to the beauty of . . . life. Because you have an opportunity to share in different backgrounds and different cultures.

"In Christ . . . Neither Black nor White"

Woody, another parish leader, concluded: So race, religion, sex, all that stuff—
it's the person that's important, and all this other stuff, it's superficial. The
diversity as a result of that comes naturally. When you start dealing with an
individual and watching them grow and helping them grow and have love
for them and they have love for you, the diversity comes naturally out of
that. . . . At this point, I think if you were to stop and actually try to *get* that
diversity, you can't do it. . . . It naturally flows, and I think [diversity] is a
sign of a healthy church. But I don't think you can make a healthy church
by making it diverse, you know?"

Participating in a community that provides the wholeness that we miss
if we hang out only with people just like us is "exciting" and "adds to life's
beauty." Members of Ascension are clear that the diversity of their church
"comes from love." They say, "God is revealed" through this diverse community gathered. This awe-filled surprise at the experience of oneness reminded our research advisory committee of the Pentecost story in Acts, a
book which itself pulls together diverse traditions. Parishioners are saying,
"Even though we have all this diversity, you can see we have one church."
They experience that it's rich, not split. Like the Church of the Ascension,
the church in Acts paradoxically finds diversity necessary so members can
see that differences don't have to separate them. Even more: as differences are held together in unity, we experience joy because all these riches
are brought together. It is *in* the diversity of gifts that the Spirit creates
unity. In this parish as in Acts, people say in wonder, "Everybody understands each other!" And: "We 'get it' precisely across the lines of difference that you might think would separate us."

Take a deep breath, right down to your middle.

As you breathe out, let all tension flow out.

Sitting aware on the edge of mystery,
With God as your companion,
notice what kinds of differences between people stand
out in your church.

What are the effects of those differences on the com-
munity?

I asked Ascension's rector, Mary Sulerud, "Are there things you do to support this gift of diversity?"

"First, of all," she replied, "as you know, there are a large number of African Americans in the congregation, and culturally, naturally, they create community around church—that is a gift they bring. There were some important supports in place when I came. The lay eucharistic ministers 'look like us' [i.e., reflect the variety of the congregation], so that brings the diversity up front. At international dinners we eat each other's food. Intentional companion relationships with churches in South Africa and Liberia have been important. More recently, in Lent, we get up and tell our stories of faith—and the success of this program reveals something about people's hunger to tell those stories. This year we plan to spend some time talking about Christianity and the various cultures and countries that come to Ascension—the gifts people bring to us. We'll include Bible study and hymns from different cultures. Having *Lift Every Voice and Sing*[1] in the pews helps.

Some interviewees at both Ascension (Silver Spring) and St. Thomas' Parish (which we'll consider next) objected because they saw the Ware instrument dividing people into categories. The reason: "People at Ascension have spent *careers* breaking out of type," said Mary Sulerud. The focus is that the separating power of differences is overcome as the Spirit creates unity in diversity.

In Ascension's story the experience of diversity as a sign of completeness in the communion of love is received as a gift. We could create a text for this story by expanding on St. Paul: "In Christ there is neither Jew nor Greek, male nor female, black nor white"—but one corporate person with diverse parts. Diversity within a corporate person is an occasion for loving celebration, not alienation or sameness. We "eat each other's food."

"In Christ . . . Neither Gay nor Straight"

The people of St. Thomas' helped me understand how they experience the corporate spiritual energy in the gay-straight diversity of their congregation.

First, listen to an interviewee describe a gay visitor's surprise. (Alban Institute research reveals that surprises are key places to look for what's important in a congregation's life, and that visitors and newcomers are often the first to pick up these clues.)

MRS. LOCKWOOD: One Sunday one of my young male friends . . . introduced me to a guest he had brought. And the guest said, "This is a wonderful place. . . . It's not just that [this church] tolerates us . . . . It accepts us, it's that it embraces us." That says it.

CELIA: So this presence of gay people really forms the church in some deep way?

MRS. LOCKWOOD: Yes. . . . And I think it must be God-driven and God-led.

Another describes how this "wonderful experience" that "forms the church" came about:

HAL: By the time I'd become senior warden, the gay presence here was significant, although it wasn't talked about. . . . And in the course of the search process, the whole question of gayness was put on the table . . . because we had to make sure that the congregation would be supportive should we choose a gay priest. . . . And this was a catalyst that started a bunch of people here in the church . . . speaking up about their gayness. . . . Well, this was a big "Aha" for me. . . . It really has broadened my humanity. . . . And dealing with these people as human beings, and seeing their strengths and their humanity, and their sameness and differentness with me, has been a very moving spiritual thing. . . . I think we're being called upon to be a model to show that it is possible to have a diverse worshiping group where gays are welcome, are part of it, and that no harm is going to result to anyone as a result of that. . . .You can just see biases falling off like needles off an old Christmas tree.

This communion of gay and straight people is in a deep way the essence of St. Thomas's spirituality. For Jim Holmes, the "sense of being loved by God is central," and that love leads to accepting all people. St. Thomas' emphasis on welcome is about creating a space that says yes to people to whom a great many nos have been said. A community is being nourished here in which that yes flows across the usual line separating straight and gay, and people see this "yes" experience as a transcendent reality, a gift, a way of being that is not simply of their own construction.

An important gift of St. Thomas' "is the gift of welcome," said Jim Holmes. "People want to be welcoming. This effort needs constant attention, especially in a parish where, of 220 adults, just this year 25 people left [because of job relocation or other reasons], and 40 came in." A lay member added: "We pay attention to people's gifts, and help people get in quickly."

Jim concluded: "I think, as well, the straight folks are here partly because they want to be in a diverse setting. They don't like . . . segregated places; they find there is some sterility to that. I think that people here genuinely see in other faces here the face of God, that they perceive other people to be brothers and sisters in God."

Take a deep breath, right down to your middle.

As you breathe out, let all tension flow out.

Sitting aware on the edge of mystery,
With God as your companion, reflect:
Do you notice any energy from diversity in your
church?

As you listen to people, do you hear anyone speaking
of an experience like seeing God in the face of the
other?

* * * * *

There is a great wisdom hidden in the old bell tower calling people with very different backgrounds away from their homes to form one body in Jesus Christ. It is precisely by transcending the [separating power of] many individual differences that we can become witnesses of God who allows his light to shine upon poor and rich, healthy and sick alike.

—Henri Nouwen, *Reaching Out*[2]

* * * * *

CHAPTER 4

A Spring for the Church's Ministry in the World

As you have sent me into the world, so I have sent them.
(John 17:18)

A s the research advisory committee pondered Ascension, Silver Spring, one member registered a surprise: despite the evident power of this congregation's spiritual life, "What is missing that puzzles and disturbs me is that I don't see any societal criticism. There are only a few tangential words about social activism, although they do mention the meeting next door of the mission committee, which is doing 'wonderful work.'" This was the moment for an "Aha!" The advisor's puzzlement surfaces an assumption: we have been used to thinking about social relevance as church-sponsored talk and task forces intended to address social issues in the world.

AN INCARNATIONAL MODEL OF CHANGE

I see Ascension showing forth a more incarnational social activism—flowing naturally from the *being* of that congregation in a way that's not just ethical; it springs from the congregation's spirit. It's not that the people of Ascension aren't doing specific missions. It's that the energy lies more profoundly in an organic form of ministry in which being and doing flow together. Annie, an African-American interviewee, sees clear signs that Ascension's diversity is an important calling for the church: "Ascension is a very inclusive church, respectful of difference at the same time as we try to be the one community. . . . With the changes in the demographics of American society, where people are going to have to work together, where people are going to have to accept leadership from all kinds of folks, Ascension is a good example of how this can work." (Her comment reminds me of Hal's "We're being called upon to be a model" at St. Thomas'.)

This church incarnates diversity as a model for a world that needs to know how diverse people can live and work together. "Social agenda" in this congregation is deeper than a principle or a plan. It's about the very *being* of this church. Members of Ascension are congruent followers of One who often began his sayings with "I am . . ." but whose being, not at all the static source of divine action, is itself congruent with the way God is and acts "for us." Social action is about what flows out when you love God and do as you please in response to that love. This sense of social ministry as not just an activist program but a reality rooted in the church's being answers the question, "Where is the social activism?" but in an unexpected way. We're called "to be this place where diversity works," which the people of Ascension see as a numinous reality, and for which Richard Chiola supplied the word *koinonia*: "It is nothing that we strive for," Chiola said. "There is no sense whatever of struggling toward this, as an ideal. It is a gift, a charism, a work of the Spirit that we incarnate." Here we are confronted with an interesting invitation to take the word "gift" seriously, even literally, but as incarnated and therefore experienced within the relationships in a congregation.

Take a deep breath, right down to your middle.

As you breathe out, let all tension flow out.

Sitting aware on the edge of mystery,
With God as your companion, notice:
Is there any way in which the "being" of your church
implies a gift of God and a call? Can you think of a
way in which the "being" of your church is not some-
thing you and others have simply constructed but some-
thing that is given to you to live?

* * * * *

There is a pervasive form of contemporary violence to which the idealist fighting for peace by non-violent methods most easily succumbs: activism and overwork. The rush and pressure of modern life are a form, perhaps the most common form, of its innate violence. To allow oneself to be carried away by a multitude of conflicting concerns, to surrender to too many demands, to commit oneself to too many projects, to want to help everyone in everything is to succumb to violence. The frenzy of the activist neutralizes his work for peace. It destroys the fruitfulness of his own work, because it kills the root of inner wisdom which makes work fruitful.

—Thomas Merton[1]

* * * * *

CORPORATE SPIRITUALITY NURTURES INDIVIDUAL MINISTRY

Congregations need to move out from what Merton called "the root of inner wisdom which makes work fruitful." I see that fruitful work, the positive impact on society, shining forth most clearly in members' individual stories—when they walk out of Ascension's doors and go to work, to live their lives in their families and communities.

Annie describes her faith at work:

I teach in the School of Social Work at Howard University. And I'm interim assistant dean for student affairs. That's how my spiritual life enters. I have to pray a lot for guidance. . . . In academia . . . there are all kinds of egos, and there is the power of knowledge. . . . You can just pray to be humble. . . . I want to make a contribution, and it's not so much for yourself but it's for the students you're working for, or it's for the clients you have to be concerned about . . . it's being able to have those values play a part without imposing them on people. . . . There tend to be groups or factions . . . and if you're not interested in being a part of that, and you just like to be you, and relate to everybody, you know that requires a certain kind of *being* in the environment. And I don't think I could have done it without a spiritual sense, without that part of my life that really has to do with how you relate to people from the janitor on. . . . Not to mention students. . . . When you're in social work . . . you have to call on strength and inner resources. And so I include spirituality in my teaching.

Ministry springs from the corporate spirituality of the congregation, and is expressed not only corporately but through the individual ministries of the parishioners. Ascension trusts laypeople to be in ministry where they are instead of letting the church set the agenda.

Here another significant surprise popped up. I had submitted an article about the story of Ascension to a respected mainline Protestant periodical. The editor raised a concern about "the social worker at Howard. At the end you say, 'How could clergy tell [the social worker] what Christian ends to pursue at Howard University . . . ?' If not the clergy, then who at Ascension is helping the social worker sort through the issues and concerns she faces in her setting and develop a spiritual approach to dealing with those concerns?"

"Oh, yes, here is another one of those surprises," I thought. It sounds almost as though this editor believes that clergy must tell Annie how to carry out her ministry in the Howard University School of Social Work. I consulted with Mary Sulerud, and wrote back to the editor:

> I know we've been socialized in mainline Protestantism in recent years to look for the "how to do it," and I've participated in that. But the learnings I'm getting from this research are saying clearly, "This isn't about techniques." It really is about "gifts." Uncertain how to proceed, I forwarded your letter to Mary Sulerud. . . . She confirmed my first reaction: "It isn't primarily about techniques." Mary replied, "I took umbrage at their response to Annie's story—'Where are the clergy?'"
> . . . I hope my revision will provide some of your clergy readers hints about supportive things to do while leaving the major emphasis on the power in Ascension's life, where I really believe it needs to be—as response to the gifts of God.

I shared some of Mary's "umbrage," having been saddened over the years by how little is expected of laypeople, how little prepared "professionals" are to hear lay words of wisdom.

As we try to understand the church's role in supporting laity in their ministries, it is important to mention the work of the Grubb Institute for

Behavioural Studies in London, and particularly Grubb chairman Bruce Reed's idea about how people "oscillate" between church and daily life. We go to church, holds Reed,[2] after having held it all together in our daily arenas of ministry all week, to "regress to extra-dependence," to be "upheld by the everlasting arms," as we are led in worship. (How many people have I heard say, "The hour of church is the one hour where I can just be"!) Think of a small child at the playground, who jumps off his mother's lap to play with the other kids in the sandbox. A scraped knee may bring him back to the lap, where a pat and a Band-Aid soon embolden him to return to the fray. As one layperson put it, "I go to church to be patted back into shape."

According to Reed's theory, if the church does its job, the fruits of this "regression" will be found in a more just community even if the church does not carry out specific social-action enterprises.[3] Listen to Annie reflecting on her participation in her church during a period when work demands pressed hard:

> Sometimes you can be so involved that you don't give yourself a chance to step back and just be a member. This has made me think a little bit more about what it means to be a member of the community. . . . So I've had time to sit in the pews. And listen. And so I think it's been helpful. . . . I feel that there's a sense that I need to be doing more. But . . . just the experience of being able to pull back was an important thing to be able to do. To come and sit and to be a member. And to be strengthened, and to experience church in another way. . . . I was not a person in the past who thought about meditation. . . . So now I know that I'll never go back to being overly involved. That I will leave a little piece, a little place, where there can be that kind of quiet.

Listening to Annie might give church leaders an idea that I suspect is often hard for them to keep in mind: we need to encourage laypeople to look at their congregational participation in the context of how it affects their spiritual growth, the way it nourishes them to meet other demands. Supporting this perspective might be one of the fruits of interviews or other kinds of conversations with laity.

In our research advisory committee discussion of this point, Richard Chiola provided a helpful summary of this question of how the church relates to the ministry of the laity, as he distinguished diverse ways of equipping the saints for change in the world. One is to bring them together for liturgy and then aim them at specific changes. I think of that way as pragmatic and functionalist. The other way is to gather them together so they become one loaf and then send them back out as pieces in their own diverse settings where they are equipped to be leaven in the dough of the world. This is a very different way. You never achieve specific ends so much as you nurture these people to be where they need to be in the midst of the world. It's a different way of doing change. It can appear that they are not particularly interested in changing social systems, but it seems to me that this is the way much more far-reaching change can be accomplished. It's like the picture of the church in Acts—they don't appear to be out to change slavery, or any particular social system, but they seem to be changing everything.

I responded: "That latter way, a more organic, perhaps more mystical, way is how I see it in these churches, trusting laypeople to be in ministry where they are, instead of the church setting the agenda in a more top-down, rationalist way. If they are transformed people, they can be trusted to go out into the world and be ministers in the workplace, neighborhood, and family which only they can know." People may find themselves more appropriately *supported* than *directed* by their church community in their daily ministries. Here is an alternative to relying primarily on denominational departments that are expected to identify and proclaim the "right" issues. I believe this more organic way could at least enrich and deepen the "social issues" model which has held sway for so long in mainline Protestantism.

Mary Sulerud's note in her final evaluation of the project and its effect on the church provides us with an appropriate last word on this subject. Thinking back over the past two years in the life of Ascension's interviewees, she concludes: "All have a commitment to new, quite different, and much more defined ministries than prior to this project, and the universal understanding by all the interviewees is that each is a seed scattered by the Spirit of God amid the soil of God's people."

Take a deep breath, right down to your middle.

As you breathe out, let all tension flow out.

Sitting aware on the edge of mystery,
With God as your companion,
picture the people leaving the altar of your church,
walking out the door, and returning to the ministries in
their daily lives.

What do you see, as you follow that image?

Do you have a sense of any springs of those ministries
in their congregational participation (of the kind that
Annie described above)?

CHAPTER 5

The Mission to Be Church in This Place

As you, Father, are in me, and I am in you, may they also be in us, so that the world may believe that you have sent me.

(John 17:21)

Now let's back off and come at "the church in the world" and "holding differences together" from another perspective. Are there different ways to be "the church in this place"?

A COMMUNAL CHURCH

Another kind of church that has its own way of holding differences together is the communal church, a *parish*, whose members are drawn from the neighborhood.

Let's get acquainted with St. Peter's in Poolesville, Maryland, a church of 347 members. We arrive at St. Peter's after an hour's drive from Washington, much of it through miles of farmland. In many ways the distance separates it from the diocesan center, and it is the only Episcopal church in town.

The early service is smaller and attended mostly by older people who like a slightly more formal service, one person tells me. As I arrive, that service is just ending, and the Rev. Steve Hayward, the rector, is standing at the door shaking hands with the children, who come out first.

Following the early service comes Bible study, today including one woman and four men, most of them getting on in years. This morning the story of Cain evokes quite a lot of conversation about the criminal-justice system, whether or not prison inmates are being rehabilitated, and how the account of God's providing Cain a mark that would protect him might relate to our way of dealing with people who commit serious crimes today. Steve's style is informal, and he invites people to connect the story to concerns in contemporary life. Aspects of his style also show up in changes to the worship space. In this 250-year-old church, with its white interior and stained-glass windows, the large pulpit has recently been removed, and a new communion table has been placed so that the Eucharist can be celebrated with the priest facing the people. Steve tells me the congregation had some tough times over changing the church furniture around. He says many people's responses occasioned an opportunity and requirement for him to take on a burden of firm leadership, in contrast to his usual collegial style.

In the service I see a number of gray heads as well as young families among the all-white congregation. There are wafers rather than loaf bread for communion, no inclusive language, and it is a rather standard middle-of-the road service.

Announcing a hymn, Steve says, "We're not going to sing what it says up there on the board. We're going to sing number 671." And then we sing "Amazing Grace." During the sermon he walks up and down the aisle. The service has, in an impromptu way, become a family service, with the children present throughout, because the basement has flooded overnight. People have been busy mopping up and piling everything on tables to keep it out of the puddles, so there is no Sunday school.

Steve begins the sermon with a very informal telling of the story of the Prodigal Son. When he tells about the younger son taking all the money and going off, he comments to the children, "I don't think your parents will like this story." He then moves on to ask the children questions. At one point, a couple of paper airplanes sail over a pew, and he immediately weaves that into his homily. At the end he opens up the discussion to adults, ending with the declaration that God is always watching for us, hoping we'll come through the door. Steve has a kind of cheery, bright, welcoming way, and people seem to respond to that.

I ask people at the coffee hour what is special about St. Peter's, especially about how it helps people grow spiritually. Bill, who has been coming to St. Peter's since World War II, says it is the service. Several people mention the education program, one mother of a toddler stressing that St. Peter's has education programs for all ages—from senior high down to preschoolers. Several mention the rector, who seems to be regarded with much affection.

St. Peter's Church had its beginning in what was then a sleepy little town in upper Montgomery County, Maryland, far removed from the life of the nation's capital. "Now," writes the parish historian, "We are no longer that community of farmers who petitioned the Diocese of Maryland for regular clergy or were served by riders coming out from the mother church at St. John's, Broad Creek." But for many years the history was full of signs of being on the edge, punctuated by statements like this: "Again the pulpit was left open for want of clergy and a salary." During the Civil War, though members had many southern sympathies, the church was commandeered as headquarters for federal troops, who damaged the building by tearing away planking for firewood and stabling horses inside the church. In the early 20th century the newly formed Diocese of Washington began giving financial support to St. Peter's Parish, but during World War II the diocese sent a discouraging note that the church would have to "get along with Lay Readers," as it had so often throughout its history. The Women's Auxiliary sewed for missions and conducted fund-raisers for the church. In the 1950s, during the tenure of the Rev. Carter Gillis, St. Peter's was able to fulfill all its financial obligations without diocesan assistance. During the 1970s, as the metropolitan area's population explosion reached Poolesville, the town's population grew from 500 to nearly 3,000. St. Peter's refurbished the church, and attendance nearly doubled, though "a toll of liturgical renewal and community changes brought the '70s to a quiet end," says the history. The parish historian goes on to note that, with the arrival of Steve Hayward, "St. Peter's undertook the construction of a brick-and-block parish hall in 1984 at the cost of $450,000. For a congregation that had so recently struggled to pay its bills, the amount was overwhelming." By 1991, however, the mortgage was retired, and the church again began to grow. The church now has 292 youth and adult members "in good standing," and 458 baptized members. On an average Sunday, 150 attend church.

St. Peter's is a communal church, "drawn from a surrounding parish," as Bruce Reed explains. If you're an Episcopalian in Poolesville, you go to St. Peter's. This type is different from the associational church, whose members are "drawn from a wide area, choosing to associate with others who share the idea that this church will endorse their convictions." Many city churchgoers may pass three churches of their denomination to reach their chosen associational church, where they can find the social activism, gay-straight community, or other characteristics they are seeking.[1] St. Peter's congregation, in contrast, includes many ways of thinking. In a sermon, Steve tells me, he spoke of the congregation's diversity and used the words "A house of prayer for all people." He is a rector who can get along well with all kinds of people. This is important because "We're the only game in town." Recently the town was deeply concerned about a sick child, and wanted "something done" at St. Peter's. Steve presided over a service of prayer and healing, lifting up the child on behalf of the town of Poolesville, more than on behalf of St. Peter's Church. The inclusiveness of St. Peter's, resulting in part from the small population to draw on in this town, means "you can't be too well defined." The church's mission statement reads "like a bushel basket," says one member, which may be the downside of a communal church. Efforts to get people to join your church are viewed with suspicion—you should *already have* a church affiliation in this town, where people have always gone to their family's church.

Some characteristics of St. Peter's are reminiscent of the English-style communal church: It is a country parish, close to nature and with a strong appreciation of the land; thanksgiving is important to the people of St. Peter's, as is a sense of "our abiding continuity" in this church with its 250-year history.

BEING "THE CHURCH IN THIS PLACE"

During the centennial year 1991, the Rev. Henry Breul, rector of St. Thomas' for the previous 26 years, included in his retirement comments these words: "I think that not having a rector in place at the centennial will allow the parish to celebrate just what it should be celebrating: the history of the people of God in this place."

"The mission to be church in this place" is an important dimension of this church's congregational spirituality. St. Peter's has its communal way of being planted in Poolesville. Associational churches have another way: people choose to attend because they want, as in the case of St. Thomas', for instance, to be part of a gay-straight communion. St. Thomas' Parish (its formal name which speaks of church *here*) has a strong commitment to its roots in this place—Dupont Circle. St. Thomas' Parish moved "from *noblesse oblige* to being the people of God in and among the people of the neighborhood and including (in fact, *being*) diverse people, not just caring for them," concluded Richard Chiola. Following the fire, "there was a conscious choice made with lots of process to stay here and to be the parish in this place," Jim Holmes explained. "The mission to be church in this place, this year, has taken the form of a venture with St. Luke's, a larger black parish, three blocks away, to explore racism." In this emphasis on the church planted *here*, we find an ancient and central focus of the church as truly incarnate in this place, which today is maintained most clearly by Orthodox thinkers. Metropolitan John Zizioulas paints a powerful picture of the church having equally deep bonds with God and (in the present cases) Poolesville or Dupont Circle: The "identity of the Church is relational. . . . St. Paul . . . speaks on the one hand of the 'Church of God' . . . and on the other hand of the Church or churches 'of a certain place' [which] . . . implies also that the Church is by definition incompatible with individualism.[2]

Take a deep breath, right down to your middle.

As you breathe out, let all tension flow out.

Sitting aware on the edge of mystery,
With God as your companion, consider:
Do you have any sense of how your church is
gathered by God to be church in this place?

The stories in this first part of the book have illustrated some of the ways congregations begin to uncover—and act out of an awareness of—their hidden spirits: their identification with the paschal mystery, with its great theme of death and resurrection, as they suffer and discover new life; their celebration of that new life in their own story, as it shines through the transparent liturgy, and as they "see Christ in the face of the other"—the other who our culture taught us was alien. We have also seen these churches acting out of their corporate center as they offer the new way of being they have received to a world that needs to be able to see it, and as they nourish people like Annie to return to their teaching (or offices or stores), empowered by the transforming spirit they sensed at the altar. The church is also called to be *the church in this place*, and we have noticed two ways these churches' hidden spirits become incarnate *right here*, in Poolesville or Dupont Circle.

I noticed another surprise at the end of the project's first year. The power of the learnings about the corporate nature of congregational spirituality was dramatized for me by the necessity of renaming the project. The original title was "Congregations Nourishing a Spirituality for the World." I had to say, finally, to the rector of St. Thomas': "The congregational spirituality that you are teaching me is much bigger than that title suggests. The name of the project needs a complete change." Spirituality is not a department of the congregation (in charge of enterprises like quiet days, prayer groups, etc.), as the original title might have implied. The project henceforth was simply called "The Congregational Spirituality Project," which at least leaves room for the *whole being*, the core identity of the congregation, its hidden spirit incarnate in its life and ministries, corporate and individual.

At the end of the first year what stood out for me as truly exciting discoveries were the learnings about the *corporate* spiritual realities of congregational life. Loren Mead commented on this aspect of the work as "virgin territory," unusually provocative "insights so early in the research."

What I was seeing, beginning to understand, and learning from the spiritual journeying of the people of God in Poolesville, in Silver Spring, and on Dupont Circle may invite congregations to a more profound level on which they may understand their life and work.

PART II

Discernment:
Who Are We Called to Be?
Where Are We Called to Go?

In the research, and in this book, we started by listening for the hidden spirit, the corporate soul of the congregation, through its members. We began to become acquainted with this congregational spirit, and to notice the special gifts of each spiritual community. The natural next question was, "Given these gifts, who are we called to be? Where are we called to go?" And so we now move into a process of discerning the answers to these two questions. But first, a preliminary question.

What Is Discernment?

Is discernment an attitude or an act? When we speak of discernment, we could be talking about a general attitude—a discerning heart, an ongoing availability to God embedded in a life of prayer. Or we might be speaking of an act—wondering what to do in a particular situation. Holding both these dimensions of discernment together is important: To connect the attitude and the act, we would be making our choices out of a discerning heart. The fruit of discernment is not exclusively the decision we made, but also what's happening in us as a whole person. We have to keep noticing, for instance: Are we entering this act of discernment with trust? Or is it really about getting somewhere (perhaps sliding into drivenness)? Discernment is not just about knowing we have weighed the data and chosen well. Discernment can't be wrapped up absolutely, because we're dealing with a living Spirit—in ourselves and in God. Our trust in God, our dependency on God, our felt need for grace may be far more important than anything we *know*. "By faith Abraham obeyed when he was called to set out" (Heb. 11:8). He didn't have the outcome wrapped up.

The foundational discernment question for congregations is: Are we being grounded in God *together*?[1] In the church, we are badly in need of ways of corporate discernment. For example, over many years, I have watched denominations struggle with difficult issues (like "Should we ordain gay and lesbian people?"), persisting year after year in the attempt to use secular parliamentary procedure to solve seemingly intractable questions—because they can't think of any other way. I can't help concluding not only that the methods are questionable but that they don't work. The issues don't get resolved, or the decisions don't stay made, or the bodies don't join together around their decisions with a sense of having truly worked their way through the questions. I have often reflected on how sad it is that we don't seek alternative (or at least additional) ways from our faith traditions.[2]

So let's move on to probe for faithful ways of discernment in church groups. To do that, it will help to look more carefully into this thought, introduced in the beginning of part I:

Spirituality is about a whole person.

The statement suggests that we must engage in discernment in a *whole-person* way that draws together thinking, feeling, our bodies, imaginations, and relationships. I have found this conviction illuminated, in a whole spectrum of ways, by some of the distinguished thinkers whose ideas have influenced this work. With their help, let's first identify some of the many dimensions of whole-person discernment and, second, pull those dimensions together as a statement of intention for this discernment work.

Gerald May suggests we pray that our discernment spring from *immediate presence in the world, directly perceiving things as they are, with our whole selves.*[3] "Perceiving" reminds us that the root meaning of "discernment" has to do with "sight"—to see with spiritual eyes, to distinguish or sort out, to go to the heart of the matter. "The eye is the lamp of the body" (Matt. 6:22), and if the eye is sound, the body will be healthy. The capacity to discern is like an eye, like a lamp.

Discernment involves *transformation, which is always a whole-person event*, including more than mind. "We do not think our way to a new way of living, but rather live our way to a new way of thinking," says retired pastor and author Howard Friend.[4] "I have become increasingly convinced that significant change occurs for individuals and organizations, including congregations, only when the unconscious is accessed and engaged. In my experience, the unconscious responds well to symbols and images."[5] These symbols can be made available in churches in many ways, including prayer, Scripture, sacraments, and our worship space.

The *discovery of meaning is a whole-person event*, less linear than intuitive in its form. You learn this when you see "in a flash that everything makes sense as soon as you go beyond reasoning," says David Steindl-Rast. At such revelatory moments, as poet T. S. Eliot recognized, you

    . . . apprehend
    The point of intersection of the timeless
    With time. . . .[6]

Our yearning for meaning naturally draws us to our imagination for resources not available through "hard data" or logic. "The spirit invites daring acts of imagination," says Robert Wuthnow.[7] And imagination helps open discernment groups to the spirit. Bible scholar Walter Brueggemann invites us to "pay great attention to the arts" as a way to see possibilities. "The work of the spirit" must include imagination—"the leading of the spirit to help us envision the world in new ways." Mime, drawing, and inner dialogue would be examples of imaginative "opening" ways appropriate for "the work of the spirit."[8] Imagination is a powerful way to open the material world to its spiritual depths. Another is action or practices.

Today people seeking for a whole-person way of being in the world are often drawn to activities such as prayer and devotional reading, and other practices rooted in their religious tradition that deepen their relationship to the sacred—as a primary way of living into their spiritual depths, says Robert Wuthnow. Because we enter into these activities with our whole selves, he concludes, "people who engage in these practices are also quick to emphasize *how deeply interlaced these activities are with other parts of their lives* [italics added]."[9] Practices and images each in their own way open us to the unity or wholeness that underlies the otherwise atomized dimensions of human life.

As individuals, and as congregations, we are in a lifelong search for wholeness. That is why we are drawn by the promise of wholeness articulated in the Gospel stories. It makes sense that Jesus doesn't allow the dimensions of human life to remain separate. Someone may come seeking physical healing and be offered forgiveness. Another asks for honor and is offered a way to serve others. We who seek to be whole persons need to pursue our search in congruent, whole-person ways, *to be whole even in our seeking.* In our search to be whole communities, an attention to process, to the way we live together, may be even more important than correct ideas. As always, the medium, discernment, is a vital part of the message.

For all these reasons, during the discernment stage of the Congregational Spirituality Project it became apparent that we, as discernment groups in the churches, are called to live out this whole-person way of being wholly present in our world. To summarize the thoughts gathered in this section: We need to root our discernment in "our whole being in God," watching out for the temptations to "know we're right," or to "domesticate God." We can pay attention to images and symbols, to imagination, and to the power of practice. We can listen from the heart, remembering that deep change seems to come about only by including the unconscious. And so, gathering for discernment, we need not be limited to sitting on chairs talking from the left brain, but can be enriched by whole-person practices such as contemplation, mime, and art. And we would also include Scripture and prayer, noticing the connections between the stories and our whole lives—not just our individual lives but also our life as "members" of our corporate body, the church. In church, as in life, we are called to love God with all our heart, soul, mind, and strength.

"THE GIFTS OF GOD FOR THE PEOPLE OF GOD"

> It is always poignant to realize that most people in our culture are so concerned with getting jobs done that they have lost their experiential connectedness with the divine mystery of life. This may get the job done, but one loses all sense of what they are ultimately being done for.[10]

In the parish discernment stories that follow, you will note that we always *begin with the gifts* of the churches revealed in the first-year interviews. (We will discuss the process of the interviews more fully in part 3.) It seems important to start with what God has given this church. The gifts provide positive energy, the empowering Spirit of God at work. But it is not easy for us to take the word "gift" seriously. We use this word commonly in churches without noticing how radically countercultural it is. First, a gift is something we are *given*. Only later is the gift something in response to which we take action. Our active, go-for-it mindset, which permeates the culture we swim in, will keep tempting us to rush immediately to doing.

We need to stop first, and learn to "tune in," notice, welcome, and embrace the gifts we have been given.[11] Then the discernment questions: "Who are we called to be? Where are we called to go?" must be answered before "How are we going to get there?" makes any sense.

We tend to demand the big picture, the complete plan, including strategic steps, right now. But discernment is often more like the headlights that may "cast only enough light for us to see the next small bit of road immediately in front of us."[12] We need to keep reminding ourselves that discernment is more a journey than a destination.

Part of this journey is simply learning to listen. While someone else is talking, we often find ourselves planning our own well-thought-out, significant contribution to the discussion. With practice, we can begin to learn just to listen now, and even to allow silence before offering our own words, so that we may open ourselves to the next glimmer of light that illuminates our path.

If I had known last year as clearly as I know today what hard work it is to keep overriding our default do-do-doing position, I would have said to the people in each church the words you have just read.

Take a deep breath, right down to your middle.

As your breathe out, let all tension flow out.

Sitting aware on the edge of mystery,
With God as your companion,
let your heart and mind open
To an awareness of the giftedness
of your congregation.

Let your mind run over your communal story,
including the hard times
and all that is special about your church family—
your own corner of the Whole People of God.

What have you as a corporate body been given
before you even think about doing anything with the
gift?

And then give thanks.

Let us move on now from this prologue, in which we have been gathering thoughts about faithful discernment, the use of "whole-person" ways, and the necessity of starting with God's gifts, not our actions, to some stories about how the project parishes tried to bring those ways into their discernment.

Here I need to issue a strong caution about how to read this section, which contains a good deal of "how we did it" material: *Don't take these designs and cut and paste them into your church. You have to do your own discerning work.* With that caution taken into your mind and heart and held firmly, however, you may learn some helpful things from the ways other churches went about their discerning. We can read others' stories and ask ourselves: "How would it be with our kind of church, our kinds of people, our special gifts as a congregation?"

We will begin with a more detailed description of the discernment process at one church, and then look at highlights of discerning in three other parishes—each of which offers us different perspectives on discernment.

CHAPTER 6

Discerning at St. Patrick's Church

S t. Patrick's mission came into being in 1911 "to serve Episcopalians in what was then the upper northwest section of Washington at the dawn of the automobile era." The mission became a parish in 1946. Under the leadership of the Rev. Tom Bowers in the 1960s, the church began to shift from being a neighborhood church to being one that involved itself actively in the life of the city, particularly in civil rights activities and the Head Start program. The 1970s saw strong parish support for women's ordination and the founding of St. Patrick's Day School, and the next years brought an expansion of the school, the building of a new church, and outreach programs focusing on ministries with Anacostia (an African-American area of the city) and, further afield, Native Americans and Haitians. Today St. Patrick's is a parish of 600 members ("people who participate in the community and are known") with an average Sunday attendance of 162.

The morning I went to church at St. Patrick's was a special youth service, and young people stood at the door greeting parishioners—very friendly, polite, and helpful. A big bulletin board displayed name tags, which people were asked to wear—and most did. As I walked in and sat down, I noticed young families gathering. Almost everyone was white. The bustling atmosphere was accentuated by the noise created by hard surfaces in the large room. A lot of children were present; as someone commented later, "They're running all over the place and nobody cares."

In the service, four children acted out the Gospel lesson about "catching fish," and the sermon picked up the theme of being a fish, feeling like a fish out of water when heading off to college. (Students, many of whom had attended St. Patrick's Day School earlier, were now about to move on to college from private secondary schools like Potomac, St. Alban's, and Sidwell Friends.) Attention to families and children is an important part of

St. Patrick's for members, and people say the community is "like a family." Everybody's birthday appears in the bulletin. The church feels informal, not buttoned-down, with a sense of "family comfort." At the offertory, kids race up and put cans and boxes of food in the offering basket. Children are welcome to remain with their families for the entire liturgy, but smaller ones can also go downstairs for their own program. I had the sense of the Rev. Betty McWhorter, the rector, as a sensitive mother presiding over this family.

At the coffee hour several people came and talked to me about "the Troubles."

THE TROUBLES

Before Betty McWhorter was called to St. Patrick's as rector three years ago, the previous priest had first divorced, then declared he was an alcoholic, and later came out as gay. A period of intense conflict ensued, and the priest was fired. Betty has interviewed all but one of the previous rectors and discovered that conflict as a form of intimacy ("one of the ways people can get nose to nose") has been a thread in St. Patrick's life throughout its history. Betty said that people were repeating the story of "the Troubles" ceaselessly when she came. Now they were worn out. They just wanted to be nourished. Corinne Ware, the member of the research advisory committee who paid special attention to St. Patrick's, concluded, "My impression is that this is a warm and exhausted parish. They are strongly self-identified as having been hurt. . . . Like cut flowers, they are wilted."

"The scriptural image I see for them is the man by the pool," Corinne reflected. Richard Chiola mused, "'I'm lying there all these years with nobody to throw me into the water.' Do they really want to be healed?" Corinne replied: "I think that they do." The church has a special openness to wounded people, who—perhaps significantly—have a high profile. The crucifer is a girl with Downs syndrome. A retarded man frequently interrupts the service. I interviewed a woman suffering great stress with two severely retarded children. These people seemed to be saying, "We are wounded— and all we have is each other." St. Patrick's is showing that it can live with wounds. Parishioners can experience intimacy without the in-your-face aspect of conflict. Instead, the fact that all is not OK is the occasion for *care* as community, though cure remains elusive.

Community seems to mean "All we have is each other." Said one interviewee: "Our whole thrust is to get people connected." Their strong need to get together and stay together seems to make members leery of dividing for Christian education on Sunday morning. The rector summarized: "People come for the community, and they stay for the community." Their charism is "the ability to be family and take care of each other," reflected Corinne Ware. "The picture of the caring is that they're leaning on each other." The woman with the disabled children can be relaxed, knowing her children will be OK here. The church puts out its arms for her.

"If they could take their caring of each other and connect it with their theology, and decide that it was worth sharing with anybody, that could be hopeful," mused one committee member. "The sense of community is created, not given," Tilden Edwards pointed out. This comment reminded Jerry May of Bernard of Clairveaux's four stages of spiritual growth. "The first stage is love of yourself for your own sake. The second is love of God for your own sake (you turn to God to get what you can). The third is love of God for God's sake, and the fourth, love of yourself for God's sake. The people of St. Patrick's are in the first stage, communally loving each other for their own sake. As long as everything is going along all right, there is no reason to move to stage two. But sooner or later they find it's not working. This church may be due for a transition"—a transition that the rector has discerned is coming.

So what kind of leadership is the rector seeking to offer this wounded parish? People at St. Patrick's are tired, and, because of all the conflict, a "generation" of leaders has not been raised up. Their customary style, which they described as "active," "involved," "doing things," has been interrupted. Betty says there is an "openness to people, yet I'm not sure they connect that [openness] with God." God-talk is not easy. The inward reach is harder than the outward reach. "They have a lock on their spiritual life," she observed. "They don't come here on Sunday morning to worship God." By participating in parish life, they have a sense of receiving something that feels vaguely connected with Sunday worship, but they don't often articulate this feeling, and it doesn't seem to have much energy. Betty sees hope in that they are "incarnational people—they come here to be incarnate in community." She wants to help them connect that human community to God.

In contrast to the traditional busy style of this church, the rector wants to wait and listen. She is a Quadrant 3 mystic on the Ware Inventory. "Hearing," "signs," and "assurance" are important words to her, and she is comfortable with patient waiting. Her maternal, hospitable style fits her sense of calling "to be a healer and reconciler." She sees that these people have a long way to go in their spiritual development." Church is something that happens between ten and 11 on Sunday morning—period. Yet some interviewees feel challenged by the probing questions in her sermons— questions that make hearers ponder: "How might this be happening in *my* life?"

St. Patrick's First Discernment Meeting

After many preparatory conversations, Betty McWhorter and I planned the following meeting. I will present our design for the meeting and intersperse the steps, as we carried them out, with some significant comments members of the group made during the meeting itself.

Introduction and Opening Prayer

I. Gifts

Betty and Celia begin with a "pump-priming" conversation about the gifts of St. Patrick's Church.

CELIA: Among the gifts I have heard from you during the interviews is community—that includes availability for others, especially in crisis, and your support for each other. And your rector, who after tough times, seems to be one who can lead you into the future, especially given the interest in deeper spirituality expressed by some interviewees.

BETTY: I would like to complement that list. I see community—which means belonging, loving, safety, welcoming, caring. People feel supported and special here. There is openness, and diversity is valued. [A retarded member] was welcomed. The cards we send out to the homebound are full of names. And people can be open.

II. Corporate Spirituality

Celia introduces the idea of corporate spirituality—a church having a soul, like a person.

Betty presents a picture of St. Patrick's as a person on a journey (she has created a bright person-on-the-move of colored paper).

She asks: "Who is this person, St. Patrick?" She writes people's an-swers on the drawing, emphasizing the gifts:

- Even though there are time pressures, the *heart* gives time to children, reaches out to others
- Accepts conflict; we can disagree
- Courage: African Americans came and changed us [this goes back to the 1960s]
- When couples are in trouble, supports both partners
- Big shoulders, no matter what is going on
- Searching, questioning
- We are a work in progress
- High-energy person!
- Busy
- Seen as affluent
- New and old persons
- Open to all

III. African Bible Study on John 5:2-9 (The Man by the Pool)

1. *Celia reads passage*

> Now in Jerusalem by the Sheep Gate there is a pool, called in Hebrew Beth-zatha, which has five porticoes. In these lay many invalids—blind, lame, and paralyzed. One man was there who had been ill for thirty-eight years. When Jesus saw him lying there and knew that he had been there a long time, he said to him, "Do you want to be made well?" The sick man answered him, "Sir, I have no one to put me into the pool when the water is stirred up; and while I am making my way, someone else steps down ahead of me." Jesus said to him, "Stand up, take your mat and walk." At once the man was made well, and he took up his mat and began to walk.

Each person identifies the word or phrase that catches his or her at-tention—and shares that word or phrase with minimal adornment

- "38 years!"
- "Taking up his mat"
- "Do you want to be made well?"
- "Excuses"

2. Celia tells the story, slowly, with the following instructions:
   Find a space for yourself in the room.

(Story is read.)
   Be a person in the story—this is just for you, a private miming.
   Be the man.
   Now be Jesus.
   How did it feel being the man?
   How did it feel being Jesus?
   *Take a moment to write a journal note on this experience if you
   like.*
   Now let's take some time to share how you felt in each role.

3. Jay (senior warden) reads the passage again.

> Now in Jerusalem by the Sheep Gate there is a pool, called in Hebrew
> Beth-zatha, which has five porticoes. In these lay many invalids—
> blind, lame, and paralyzed. One man was there who had been ill for
> thirty-eight years. When Jesus saw him lying there and knew that he
> had been there a long time, he said to him, "Do you want to be made
> well?" The sick man answered him, "Sir, I have no one to put me into
> the pool when the water is stirred up; and while I am making my way,
> someone else steps down ahead of me." Jesus said to him, "Stand up,
> take your mat and walk." At once the man was made well, and he took
> up his mat and began to walk.

*Each writes down "what this passage touches in our [St. Patrick's] life
today."*

All read what they have written.

HARRIET: Hearing people say "Jesus empowers us" [leads me to ask]: What
   is St. Patrick's illness? If we took that step [of knowing our illness and
   Jesus' empowering], we'd be healed.
DONNA: I felt impatience—then empowerment. Almost as though I were
   waiting for others to have the answer, but the answer is in ourselves.
   What is needed? To be whole, empowered.
BETTY: We tend to be dealing with excuses: too few people, can't teach,
   don't have time for choir, our past was rocky—a theology of scarcity.

We are hesitant to meet Jesus face to face. I see our hesitancy, like that man. Others outside this community see our strengths and are amazed and marvel at the life and vibrancy here.

KATHRYN: I am amazed that we didn't mention the 38 years. Don't keep going back to how you got to this miserable state.

JANE: We are called to notice more of each other—to notice others' courage. . . . We don't have to always come from scarcity. We can learn to center and do more with less. We have so much creativity.

JAY: The sick man was in only one "portico." This conversation is taking place in only one portico of St. Patrick's. How wonderful to carry the message into other parts of our life! All you need to know is what you want to do and then do it.

MILLY: I feel like we get very stuck in our lives, thinking of ourselves in one box. Break out of it!

JERRY: How close to a 38-year cripple are we?

4. Celia reads the passage as a meditation. "I'm going to suggest that you put yourself in the story, as this person-who-is-St. Patrick's." [Reads the story again, ending just before Jesus speaks.]

Now in Jerusalem by the Sheep Gate there is a pool, called in Hebrew Beth-zatha, which has five porticoes. In these lay many invalids—blind, lame, and paralyzed. One man was there who had been ill for thirty-eight years. When Jesus saw him lying there and knew that he had been there a long time, he said to him . . .

"Jesus is about to speak. What does he say to you? Carry on the dialogue with Jesus in your own way, as St. Patrick's. . . ." [Silence] "Take a few minutes after the silence to journal briefly about what you said and what you heard."

All share:

MARY JANE: If you can't go down the ramp [to the pool], find another way.

DONNA:
    JESUS: "You can do it."
    ME: "How?"
    JESUS: "Through prayer."
    ME: "How do I do that?"
    [Silence.]

MILLY: My dialogue:
>   JESUS: Before you get up and move forward, you need to recognize
>   what has brought you to this moment. You can't let the past continue to
>   cripple you, and you can't forget it.

BETTY: Jesus became Dr. Seuss.
>   Jesus sat down beside St. Patrick.
>   I thought of the [Dr. Seuss] book.

[Here Betty acts out Jesus/Dr. Seuss reading to St. Patrick's.]
>   Sit very quiet.
>   "O the places you'll go!"
>   The five porticoes.
>   The people you'll reach, if you just get up!
>   Where have you not gone yet?
>   "O the places you'll go!"

JAY: Fear of the unknown is a major reason why St. Patrick's hasn't
>   [moved]. . . .

HARRIET: I began to stretch a little and see strengths. The beginning of the
>   exercise was wonderful. I began looking at my strengths. What does
>   standing up mean for St. Patrick's? [This could be an important ques-
>   tion for the future.] We have strengths, we can walk.

DONNA: There's a lot of creativity, a lot of reluctance.

BETTY: *[noting that the meeting is drawing to a close]* In the profile it
>   said St. Patrick's was looking for a "spiritual leader" and [that the
>   church was ready] to get up and walk in that direction. I am grateful
>   that you are willing to sit, listen, pray. That's a gift! You have no task
>   now [in this meeting]. I see this place hungry for adding to our life.
>   Many of us said St. Patrick's was quiet, talking to Jesus. People in the
>   ten o'clock service asked for silence. This must be a ripple effect.
>   Thank you. Keep listening.

*Closing: Betty leads closing prayer, ending by asking people to keep
this discernment process in their prayers.*

Here are some of Betty's "musings" after the meeting:
>   The feeling of lack of competence underlies much of what has kept us
>   from getting up and walking. . . .There are not enough deep spiritual
>   roots around in the community to nourish and grow some really good
>   stuff while keeping us grounded. Maybe what we need is some time

and effort on "root tending." [*About the response to the Bible study:*]
I wonder if this might be an awakening that it really is up to the people
of St. Patrick's to get up and walk, whether that walking be down the
path of education, spiritual growth, outreach, [or] worship. Given the
history of the community's system—that of being a very rector-cen-
tered and rector-driven community—and given the reality of the current leadership (a rector who believes that life must come from the
community if it is to be sustained and deepened), this might be right on
target. . . . I wonder if we don't need to build on the feeling of compe-
tence and responsibility for the community . . . coupled and strength-
ened with the joy which comes from experiencing walking into new
places. . . . Given the busyness of the community, there are lots of
reasons why it is not convenient to get up and walk . . . also it might be
a little bit frightening. . . . there is the potential to wobble and stumble
and even fall!"

Betty and I later had a substantial and helpful talk about the meeting,
the comments from the advisory committee meeting (which she found full
of pregnant ideas), and her own meditation on it, which she titled: "What is
God saying to me about St. Patrick's?"

* These are my children in whom I am well pleased.
* Care for them. They are hurt and tired and need a shepherd to love
  them to life.
* They require a lot of patience and love.
* They are scared. You are asking them to go places unknown, and to let
  go of being in control.
* I want them to learn about the gentle strength which lies within
  each one.
* I want them to come to know me and love me.
* I want them to come to know I know them and already love them.
* They will never ever be completely satisfied—and for that I am glad!

"We have trouble staying in the present," Betty later reflected, "but we
might take our cues from the children, who seem to be more open to the
present than consumed by the future." This seems an appropriate vision for
a congregation where children have an important place, and the vision might
also reflect the playfulness that was evoked in the discernment meeting.

Betty reports new hopefulness, more involvement and investment of people, signs of new life in the congregation: "We *are* walking. . . . I see in Jay [the senior warden] and the lay leaders a strength and knowledge that *they* are the church. Not the priest or the building. [People are] going into the water, walking down the steps."

REFLECTIONS ON THE ST. PATRICK'S DISCERNMENT PROCESS

A wounded church like St. Patrick's may be particularly encouraged by beginning the process with a description of the parish's *gifts*. Every church discernment meeting began with a picture of the gifts I had heard through the interviews, so this list of gifts is nothing imposed, but the simple product of listening. (The people who came to the discernment meetings were primarily the interviewees who had taught me about their church's gifts.) And in the meeting the participants were invited to "edit" the description of the gifts.

To the gift of "community," which I reflected back to the St. Patrick's folk at the beginning of the meeting, I would, following the meeting, want to add one more gift: These are people who can get into a discernment process with their whole selves—not just head, but also heart, soul, and strength. People were very open to *experiencing* the story: in working with the drawing of St. Patrick, in their miming in response to the Bible passage (first being the man who had been ill for 38 years, then being Jesus), in their meditations (moving from the story into a conversation with Jesus).

Looking at the parish as a "corporate person" is key,[1] and drawing and describing St. Patrick's as a person-on-a-journey provided a helpful way of inviting people to flesh out their picture of that person. This simple game gives people a way to think about their church's corporate spirituality— something they may have never thought about before. (It was Betty McWhorter who first had the idea of using a "homicide outline" drawing to picture the parish person, and then filling in the outline drawing of St. Patrick with the people's comments. This idea was picked up by some other church groups in the project.)

Three of the churches in the project engaged in an African Bible Study[2]—a sort of contemporary form of *lectio divina* (a classical method of praying with a biblical selection at deepening levels), in which we return to a Scripture selection from a number of points of view, noticing what captures our attention, how it relates to our experience, and how it suggests what we might be called to be or do. I believe this is a powerful and effective way to engage with the Bible—connecting the story in a profound, whole-person way with our lives (in this case, our corporate life). Every time we read the passage, people can go deeper in their perception of that connection. The method invites us into prayer. In one case, a Scripture passage that seemed to speak to a congregation arose out of the silence in a research advisory committee meeting, and I then suggested it to the rector during our planning session.

In the project churches this kind of Bible study specifically encourages people to explore how our corporate spirituality is revealed in our story and to discern how we might be called to live in response to the invitation discerned in the passage. At St. Patrick's I sensed, and Betty confirmed, an adventurous attitude toward whole-person methods, which invited us to build into the process the further dimensions of mime and a meditation extending the conversation with Jesus. It was clear that miming is an especially valuable whole-person way; people can go beyond the *idea* of St. Patrick's before Jesus by venturing to come to that meeting with their whole and responsive bodies. I suggest ending the meeting by inviting people to pray for the church and each other, and to promise to continue that prayer until the next meeting.

We will see that congregations have a range of openness to such whole-person methods. As a result of observing that variety, I would suggest *inviting* churches to venture right to (or slightly beyond) the boundary of their place of comfort with whole-person ways that are unfamiliar to them, without putting pressure on them. This work in the planning team with the rector as partner (or, as at Ascension, Lexington Park, with a larger planning team) was a delicate place of discernment for me as the spiritual companion, relying on a close partnership.

I believe it is useful to remember that there will be introverts and extroverts present in the discernment. Brief opportunities for journal-writing during the meeting time will discourage excess rambling off the top of the head, diminish possible domination of the meeting by the extroverts, and offer the introverts processing time so that they can offer their gifts to the others.

It was Betty who discerned the most fruitful role for her to take in this meeting. Though we planned the meeting collegially, she asked me to take a more primary leadership role than is my usual practice, so that she could, as she put it, "play with the people." Betty's playing alongside her people was the most *encouraging* choice we could have made for her role. (Play is an often-forgotten whole-person activity. Think for a moment about the contributions of the playful elements in the meeting—such as the bright paper St.Patrick's-on-the-move or Jesus/Dr. Seuss as storyteller.) The wide range of experiences I had with the churches in regard to choice of leadership leads me to conclude firmly that the question "Who leads?" should be answered by the criterion "What choice will serve this discernment process best?"

In general, I see signs that the people of St. Patrick's were enabled to identify their "stuck" place, and hear and articulate a call to venture out of it. Of course, this was just one meeting. We did have a smaller meeting later, with the theme "Where is God inviting St. Patrick's to walk?" which followed up on the first meeting in some useful ways. The quality of the rector's prayer for the congregation, as in the meditation on page 67, is a vital ingredient. And I hope, pray, and believe that the ongoing process of life at St. Patrick's is moving toward healing.

With thanks to St. Patrick's for sharing its initial discernment process with us, let's move on to look at how the process unfolded in three other churches.

CHAPTER 7

Discerning with the Angel of Ascension, Lexington Park

The Church of the Ascension, Lexington Park, Maryland, is a couple of hours' drive south of Washington, D.C., but still part of the diocese. When I talked with the rector, the Rev. Rona Harding, before visiting, I learned that Lexington Park has undergone much change, becoming considerably more urban than in its early days. "There are many more urban programs ministering to the poor populations that engulf our church," she said. And a large military installation is the church's neighbor.

Ascension has been through tough times. Rona told me that not long ago a group of people from Ascension left to go to another Episcopal parish. They wanted her to condemn the bishop's policy of ordaining gays and lesbians, and she would not. It has been a difficult time for her and for the church. Pledges have been down. "We didn't think we could survive," she said. "We'll make it—it's very tough on the parish, but people love each other." The period of the project coincided with the time in the church's life when this grief was most intensely felt, and then apparently less so.

Driving past Solomon's Island on my way to visit Ascension, I was aware of the Patuxent Naval Air Station as a primary setting. Ascension, which calls itself "the church with the beautiful gardens," is surrounded by lovely plantings, with bushes and holly and flower beds. Entering the church that Sunday morning, I had the sense of a middle-class, white, fairly young congregation, and an atmosphere of cheerfulness. The service was a rather traditional morning prayer service, which is held once a month. The choir was full and enthusiastic. A male lay reader read most of the lessons, so that there was a balance of male and female voices in the leadership.

Ascension is over 50 years old. Its history has been chronicled by its two rectors. The first rector, the Rev. Charles R. Daugherty, wrote a parish history describing the birth of the mission in 1949. A small group worshiped in the office of the Cedar Park Trailer Park for more than two years. An altar made out of a box, filled with all the essentials for worship, was placed against the wall during the week. On Sundays the altar guild would empty the box, put the altar in place, "and in a half-hour a place of singular beauty had been created," Daugherty recalled. Seminarians from Virginia Seminary took turns leading services. It "took some doing" to get Bishop Angus Dun of the Washington Diocese to approve the establishment of a mission church in Lexington Park. Finally he agreed, sending Daugherty to be in charge. The church, which cost $40,000, the gift of the people of the diocese, was built on a wooded lot and dedicated in 1954. Daugherty is remembered today as a priest who taught about the agape love of Christ. The church held an evangelical revival in the 1970s in which healing services attracted people from throughout the country.

Rona Harding came to be rector in 1988 after Father Daugherty retired. Interviewees stress that she is a loving person who emphasizes social action. (On the Ware inventory, Rona's responses fell mostly in the Head Spirituality and Kingdom Spirituality quadrants, 1 and 4, while laypeople responded in the Head and Heart Spirituality quadrants, 1 and 2.) She sees the core ministries of Ascension as "Christian education, pastoral care, prayer, social outreach, music, study, and worship." Under her leadership Ascension has responded to the needs of victims of hurricanes, and has sent an annual medical mission team to Honduras. Locally Ascension is the model church for a program for addicts. It has a hotline for the poor called HOPE working out of its building, and it supports a homeless shelter and a food pantry. Within the church, Ascension stresses Christian education for all ages.

In 1995 the church was rocked by controversy over the Bishop Ronald Haines's policy of ordaining practicing gay and lesbian people, and when Rona persisted in her support for the bishop, 30 out of 130 "pledging units" (couples, families, or individuals) walked out. Interviewees described the controversy as "devastating," and "like a death in the family." Remaining parishioners stepped forward to lead the Sunday school and social-outreach programs and to sing in the choir. The mourning seemed less intense during the second year I met with the people of Ascension.

The question of how to work most fruitfully with this church led to some prayerful pondering on my part. Since in the interviews "Sam," the incumbent senior warden, talked enthusiastically about himself and Rona as a "tcam," I thought it might be useful to work as a team on the upcoming discernment meeting, and suggested that to Rona. She responded that Margaret had just been elected the new senior warden, so the four of us became the leadership team. I think that was a useful way to proceed, though it was complicated, because Lexington Park is almost two hours from Washington, and we had to pursue the team approach via e-mail and conference calls. I particularly wanted a structure that would empower them to claim ownership of the process, which, at the beginning, they seemed to expect me to take.

They asked me to lead the discernment meeting (to which interviewees and a few parish leaders were invited), and the following draft plan outlines my initial proposal for a meeting design. They found some features too "far out," and I responded with a revised plan in an effort to accommodate their objections. Here is the draft plan, with some of the responses it evoked in the leadership team and in the meeting itself:

THE DRAFT PLAN

I presented some ideas for a meeting at Ascension, Lexington Park, in these "Notes to the "Leadership Team":

Rona's enthusiasm about Walter Wink, whose well-known Bible-study methods are described in Howard Friend's *Recovering the Sacred Center*, (a primary resource I shared with the rectors in the project, and which Rona found especially helpful), set me to rereading Wink's *Transforming Bible Study*.[1] I worked with pages 145-147 especially.[2] I have some concern about asking people to read the letters to the churches from Revelation because they are mostly full of judgment. I think it will help our process if we focus more on gifts than judgment. One of the powerful features of Wink's methods is the inclusion, not only of the usual sitting and discussing, but also acting out parts, drawing, and miming, which can help us to enter in at a powerfully deeper level—with not only our minds, but our hearts and spirits as well. *Consider what will allow this group we're expecting to stretch some in that direction, but will not push them too far.* I believe we will, for our purposes, do well to set aside any formal study of the biblical text, because of the short time available and the clarity of our purposes. As you look over this plan, ask yourself whether this design seems to fit, and also ask: What part would you feel comfortable leading? (Remember that we are a leadership team here, and that I am responding to your wish that I draft a possible plan for our meeting.)

The Draft Design

1. Ascension's Gifts

A. *Begin the meeting with a pump-priming discussion among the four of us:* What are Ascension's special gifts? Here are some headings for the gifts I think of, based on the interviews:

- *Love* (which needs to be defined). Subheads of love might include:
    - Social action
    - Inviting new people
    - Christian Education

B. *After a short time, open up the discussion to all present.*

2. Ascension's Angel

"In the book of Revelation, the 'angels' of the churches represent the inner nature, the 'within' of a church, its 'spirituality or essence or corporate personality.' Having listened to all these gifts of Ascension, let's try to describe Ascension's angel."[3]

A. *Describing our angel.* Draw on a very large piece of newsprint or brown paper an outline of an angel, titled "Ascension's Angel." The leader writes up characteristics of this "angel" volunteered by group members—emphasizing the gifts, but not resistant to listing an occasional problematic area.

B. *Pictures of our angel.*

1. *Drawing*: Have art supplies available. Find a quiet place in the room, and get a sense of the angel of Ascension. When you are finished, using crayons, markers, and chalk, draw a portrait of the angel of Ascension. Wink says: "Try to let the colors choose you. The pictures can be abstract, stick figures, or just pure colors. Nobody cares what they look like."[4]

2. *Share the pictures.* "Try to discern emerging common features."[5] List them on newsprint.

C. *Letters to our angel.* "Take pen and paper and go find a place in the room with enough space in front of you to fall down on your face."[6] (*This feature was later removed at the strong suggestion of the team*.) The leader reads Revelation 1:9-11a and 12-17. After verse 17a, the leader says, "Ask yourself what in you needs to die in order to receive the message of the Son of Man to the angel of [Ascension.]"[7] Pause, then complete the reading (through verse 19). Pause. Then the leader says, "When you are ready, begin to write what the son of Man says to the angel of your church."[8]

3. Meditation

When all are through writing, begin a guided meditation: Visualize the Son of Man "walking in the midst of your church, seeing everything *[silence]*. See his supernal light filling every corner of the buildings, every cell of each person. See it bathed in divine light *[silence]*. Visualize that light becoming more and more intense, transforming the whole church *[silence]*. Trust that God can actually bring this miracle about *[silence]*. Trust God for it in advance, and begin to live out of this vision of the church transformed *[silence]*. Let go of all responsibility to change your church yourself. Praise God for bringing it about *[silence]*. Amen."[9] (Be sure to leave silence between each sentence. Let the amount of silence be guided by the experience of the church with silence. Use your watch, or count slow breaths—about seven is one minute.)

4. Noticing Common Themes

"Share letters to the angel and anything else people wish to share, again seeking common threads or the authentic word of God to the congregation."[10] As themes with a lot of energy emerge, note, where appropriate, on newsprint under the heading *"Callings/Yearnings."*

5. In Closing

Ask people to pray for the church, for the discernment process in the interim before the next meeting. Pay particular attention to common threads or particularly energized themes from today.

[End of design]

(Note to the leadership team: Please respond to all of us: What seems on target? What seems not on target for the group we expect? We need a volunteer to type up a summary, run it by the rest of the team for input, and then distribute it to the members of the group.)

Here are the "Yearnings," hinted at by the common, energized themes that the session evoked, which the Ascension discernment group asked to have listed at the end of the meeting:

Reaching in:
- Yearning for more intimate relationships with others.
- Yearning for more organized small group ministry.

Reaching out:
- Yearning for more intentional outreach to the people we serve.
- Yearning for a larger group of parishioners, for we wish to share what we have with others.
- Yearning to reach the people of the community in which we serve and invite them into our worshiping community.

The first discernment meeting appeared to be energized. People contributed to the description of their Angel with gusto, and appeared to enjoy creating and sharing their pictures of the Angel and letters to the Angel. (I might generalize that, if there are evangelical elements in a parish, as at Ascension, Lexington Park, the congregation is accustomed to attending directly to the transcendent, and that will affect your decisions about methods. Be sensitive to the culture of the congregation. If the people are shy about God-talk, let your planning take that into account.) People did note that they were "still feeling some pain over those who left," and "still feeling some pain over the direction of the diocese."

Rona closed the meeting with prayer. She volunteered to share the notes she had taken with us all. She stayed up late to type the notes, and e-mailed them to the rest of the team. Later she described the meeting in an article in the parish newsletter and asked for responses from other parishioners. Following a second discernment meeting a few months later, Rona wrote, "I hope to have a parish retreat, which may be planned in the spring," and "We are following up on the neighborhood choir school and nontraditional services for the youth in the community" (initiatives which grew out of the "yearnings" above).

CHAPTER 8

Discerning at St. Peter's:
"Stay Open to Surprises!"

A s at the other churches, the Rev. Steve Hayward, the rector, and I reviewed the gifts of St. Peter's Church that had been surfaced in the first year's interviews, and together created a plan for the discernment meeting. In the middle of the meeting, to which Steve and I had brought a list of St. Peter stories to suggest for the African Bible Study, Kathleen, a group member, surprised us by suggesting we use the "Mary and Martha" story. People seemed to agree, and so we did use that story. Here's how the meeting went, as we worked with the story:

STEVE: How is God inviting us to be or change? Take two minutes silence.
    [Silence follows.]
KATHLEEN: St. Peter's has plenty of Marys, but they're all private. People come here to "do the Martha." It's as though we said, "You should mind-read my Mary part." It might help someone who is searching if we shared it. But this hasn't been our custom as a community. . . . Jesus didn't go to that house not expecting to be fed. It's all there [fixing meals and sitting at his feet]. We don't talk about our Mary part because it's too personal. We could be more articulate by saying, "This is the work God has given me."
[As we moved on toward the closing prayer]:
STEVE: Offer a petition for St. Peter's that we might need to hear.
KATHLEEN: That we may speak out loud.

When I told Chuck Olsen, the advisory committee member who paid special attention to St. Peter's, about the surprise switch of stories, he replied:

An evidence of the presence of the Spirit often is revealed when a "strange twist" takes place in the process. I saw that in the selection of the Martha [and] Mary story, which was outside your planning [and] prediction. That was the "moment" in the meeting in which a new dance began. Many leaders would have ignored it and moved on with their preplanned map. But the moment leaves leaders vulnerable, a bit out of control, and caught off guard. I think your glance and Steve's response and initiative revealed the movement of the Spirit in your midst. . . . Going with the Mary [and] Martha story took the group into the conversational arena of quiet faith [and] active faith and to the themes that we had considered when we asked each other in the research advisory committee if it would be possible for the people at St. Peter's to move into reflection on their experience within a framework of spirituality.

"Martha" was with us at the second discernment meeting, too. People kept saying in one way or another, "If other people would just help more, we wouldn't have to be so busy."

Boo: Ask more people to help. Just ask.
Celia: If others would help, it would mean there would be more "Mary time" for you?
Steve: If we get more help, we'll do more things.
Frank: We are who we are. [It's going to be hard to change this pattern.]

* * * * *

Martha would have had to let go of her own plans and ideas and achievements and simply 'hang loose' in unpredictable readiness and available to do not her own, but God's idea of her work.

—Carolyn Gratton, *The Art of Spiritual Guidance*[1]

* * * * *

Steve posed the challenge: "My expectation of St. Peter's is that its main purpose is as a spiritual community. Do people walk away with their spiritual life deepened or not?"

At its next meeting, the research advisory committee discussed the process at St. Peter's and began to mine some of its meanings—particularly the surprise in the meeting and the power of story. Chuck Olsen began our discussion by telling St. Peter's story. Then others jumped in.

CHUCK: Here was a *moment*—how do you savor a moment and invite people to unpack that moment as the Spirit inviting people to the edge? If you came back to them with an initiative, that would be resisted, but there are enough clues in this dialogue that they have a capacity to begin to go deeper with their stories and reflect on them. . . . Take them where they are and go deeper.

JERRY: I think that's where the story helps—people might disclose in story a lot more than they would in answer to "What's going on inside you when you pray?" or some question like that.

CELIA: The story could be almost a parable, laid alongside their experience.

After the second discernment meeting at St. Peter's I wrote a letter to Steve that ended: "Given your gifts, what is God calling you to be/do now? . . . Are there some ways that God may be calling you to deepen a 'Mary' kind of attentiveness?" The project evaluation, at the end of the two years,[2] provided an opportunity to discuss this question further and to deepen my understanding of how Steve's own spiritual journey was interwoven with that of the congregation's. Here are some of his responses to the evaluation questions:

1. *What role do you think your participation in the Congregational Spirituality Project has had in the development of your church's spirituality?*

   Primarily as a motivator. We were stumbling along, looking for a way to get started. Our conversations gave us a boost and a forum for getting the discussion going.

2. *What have been the most important learnings for you in the Congregational Spirituality Project?*
   - Just how deep our reluctance to talk about our spiritual life has grown
   - The desperate need we have to open up the conversation
   - To realize how our "busyness" has allowed us to avoid the contemplative side of our spiritual living

(I asked Steve about this word "desperate" when we met for a subsequent conversation. He said, "'Desperate' reflects my own feeling about where we are as a church. I feel we need to improve our spiritual life.")

CELIA: This sounds like an opening about where you are with this.

STEVE: Yes. I'm 50. There is a change in my own spiritual life reflected in this. My prayer life has taken a little bit of a new turn. My way is usually brief prayers all day—this has increased. I say the Lord's Prayer at the end of the day. It's a corporate prayer. *Our* Father. I close the day with that.

3. *What parts of the project do you feel have been most helpful? Least helpful? Rank from +4 (most helpful) to -4 (least helpful).*
    (a) *Interviews* +4. Called our people to formulate some statement about their spiritual life.
    (b) *Our individual conversations* +3. Helped give me focus on the possibilities and prevented me from getting too overwhelmed.
    (c) *Discernment process* +1. A challenging process for those of us who have been reluctant to look deeply into spiritual matters. It awakened some hearts.
    (d) *Other:* I believe that the people involved have all grown in the experience and will be better leaders in our spiritual life. They will carry that into worship leadership, as well.

4. *Can you see any effect that the [interview] experience has had on the interviewees?*
    Very important. All either felt challenged or felt they were allowed a forum to speak of their frustrations in our parish life.

In our closing conversation, I asked Steve, "What would you like me to pray for or about at St. Peter's?" Steve replied, "What we need—are 'desperate' for—is an opening up of our spiritual life to each other. This needs to be prayed for. Maybe not focus so much on the needs of the world right now."

And I continue to hold them in my prayers.

CHAPTER 9

Ascension, Silver Spring: How Are We Called to Be?

As we consider discernment at Ascension, Silver Spring, we will explore more deeply Mary Sulerud's vision of her leadership. Perhaps you remember her words:

> It's almost as though we're at the Eucharist and the window is thrown open to heaven, and there is all that holiness that stands up one side of that window and there is all that holiness that is potential and real and broken on the other, and my job is to keep working with myself and others, and to keep yoked together, so that one day those images are the same.

Returning to Mary's interview, let's listen as she expands on her vision.

MARY: Do I have a sense of being "carried"? Of course . . . every day since I've been in . . . the parish ministry, I take out the directory and I pray my way through the list of the members of the congregation every week. . . . And sometimes that's just a litany. . . . Sometimes it's really to be reminded of where that person fits into a relationship to me, or this place or their lives . . . or to be inspired by a calling that I sense God may be giving them. It's to have the folks who are here in front of me . . . with me every day, every week. That's one piece and the other [is that] I couldn't have a prayer life without Post-it Notes—folks that just ride with me every day inside the prayer book—the office book.

CELIA: What can you tell me about the connections between your relationship with God and your spiritual leadership in the congregation?—and you have begun to describe that.

MARY: Well *[long pause]*, I think there is one more piece that I didn't share, and I've shared it with people here, in the pulpit. . . . I've just really been a person who's always received a very coherent vision of what I've been called to a place to do. . . . Just after I was ordained to the priesthood [I had] a very powerful dream of what my whole vision would look like, until I died. . . . I feel really blessed because I have this sort of compass, if you will, of understanding, of apprehending, of having been drawn into some clarity about this. And it doesn't say a move to the left or a move to the right—it's not that specific. . . .

The one I received about this church was at my lowest. I don't know how aware you are of how low things were when I came. . . . And what was amazing was—I remember the night because it was about three years ago to the day, when I was interviewed by them. . . . I had such a vision of these people and the building that God was doing here that had nothing and everything to do with me. . . . I have an accountability to God to do all in my power to make it possible for them to choose to be faithful and not faithless . . . . It was simply a dream about walking into this church and it was full of people. Second, I walked through the parish hall. And there was cacophony, the incredible sound of people sawing, building, drilling, and pounding, and the smell of hot tar on the roof, wide-open doors that were there and not there, and my then junior warden walking through with a big smile on his face. And I went up to them, and I was delighted and really angry, and I said, "When did this happen, and why didn't anybody tell me?" You know, the usual way with a rector. . . . It was such a lesson to me never to underestimate what's going on, to always assume more is there. . . . That's the mystery of the Eucharist, of every sacrament we do. . . . It ended with my going into the church, being lifted high into that church in utter rapture. . . . So that is what I have come to serve. And it's important that it will be somebody else's turn [to lead this parish].

CELIA: Do you have a sense that this congregation has had an effect on your spiritual growth?

MARY: Oh, yeah, I think they have shoved me to experiment, to open myself up, to listen . . . to honor what was either unknown or really hard for me to do. They pushed me to be utterly honest about where I am coming from. They have shoved me liturgically. They have shoved me in terms of proclamation. They have shoved me in terms of being willing even when I am terrified to take steps, because if I don't, how can I ask them to?

CELIA: Can you spell out the vision a little more? Before you came, I think sometimes that they felt they had become one of the discards, as communities go.

MARY: And whether they lived or whether they died didn't seem to be of any consequence to many people—only themselves. But it's of great consequence to God, and I think they know that now.

CELIA: Yes.

MARY: And I don't think they feel despised and rejected now. At least I think they feel sure that God loves them. If I walk out of here not having done or been able to communicate anything other than that, or learned anything else myself other than that, I think I can say I'm satisfied, I'm content.

CELIA: What's it like for you to have this kind of conversation?

MARY: What this conversation does is pull me out of worrying so much that it's August 26, and out of the ten calls I said I'd make for the fundraising, I've set up only one. And take a deep breath and get some perspective on this thing.

I want to underline a few important understandings I hear revealed in this conversation—crucial attitudes that appropriately undergird a pastor's vision. First, she is clear that spiritual growth is not limited to laypeople, and that it happens in a relationship of mutuality. Second, Mary understands that "More is going on than you know." Third, she has a clear sense that her ministry is part of a longer history. Her ego is in the right place. And finally, her clarity about her foundational hope joined with her sense of organic and mutual relationship with those she calls her "partners on the plow team" helps her live out the vision with her people faithfully.

Are there other aspects of this conversation that you would like to notice especially, and perhaps use as a meditative path to your own reflections on your calling?

⌒

Take a deep breath, right down to your middle.

As you breathe out, let all tension flow out.

Sitting aware on the edge of mystery,
With God as your companion, consider:
What are some connections between your sense of re-
lationship with God and your spiritual leadership in
the congregation?

Do you have a sense that this congregation has had an
impact on your spiritual growth?

⌒

BEING AND DOING, DISCERNMENT AND PLANNING

Attending to being while doing was an important focus of the Ascension discernment group. In so many ways the life of this congregation emphasizes *being*. This is countercultural, a vital complement to our often pragmatic way of approaching parish life. With many of the churches, I had to keep saying: "Listen first and then plan." Sometimes this was very difficult for action-oriented leaders to take in, because they quickly became anxious that "we may never get anything done here." Richard Chiola commented that so often in congregations "outcomes are action oriented. . . .But the contemplative piece is always most in danger of being lost . . . because it is most often understood as the opposite of action or even something that leads to action. But contemplation is its own activity and outcome."

Ascension, Silver Spring, was a good example of a church that consciously put being before doing, in a way that was remarkable in the midst of a major building project. Let's join Mary and the discernment group in the middle of their meeting. We asked them to think about Ascension as a "person-on-a-journey" as they listened to this passage from Ephesians, which Mary had chosen and I had enthusiastically agreed would fit for the African Bible study. *(The words members of the group referred to are italicized for easy reference.)*

I have heard of your faith in the Lord Jesus and your love toward all the saints, and for this reason I do not cease to give thanks for you as I remember you in my prayers. I pray that the God of our Lord Jesus Christ, the Father of glory, may give you a *spirit of wisdom* and revelation as you come to know him, so that, *with the eyes of your heart enlightened, you may know what is the hope to which he has called you*, what are the riches of his glorious inheritance among the saints, and what is the immeasurable greatness of his power for us who believe, according to the working of his great power. God put this power to work in Christ when he raised him from the dead and seated him at his right hand in the heavenly places, far above all rule and authority and power and dominion, and above every name that is named, not only in this age but also in the age to come. And he has put all things under his feet and has made him the head over all things for the church, which is his *body*, the fullness of him who fills all in all [Eph. 1:15-23; italics added].

Each person identified the word or phrase that caught his or her attention Then followed this conversation:

ANNIE: The passage as a whole captures the faith, and what is possible when faith abides—the immeasurable power of collective faith. "Eyes of your hearts enlightened": by the diverse experiences, the need for the church to be in the world, our hearts are enlightened by each other's stories. Staying in touch with the heart.

MARY: I think of my calling to this community, understanding and embracing the hope to which we are called, not our own feelings of optimism.

CELIA: "You may know what is the hope": I see you as very hopeful people. You've come through the exodus to new life. You are very conscious of God's gifts to you, and you are grateful for what God has done. You do things based on faith. You are on the move, looking forward. And you are generous people. Let's read the passage again.

Then, *"From what I've heard and shared, what does God want us to be or do now?"*

Any sense of that?

CONNIE: We've been taking some big steps—the building fund. This person (Ascension) needs to pray for the spirit of wisdom to integrate all these transitions.

MARY: As I think about our lives, we are taking a big step. We have to be focused. It's easy to get caught up in the practical physicality of building. Keep us understanding that this step is as spiritual as physical. We need to keep praying, stay funny and playful (when it is easy to get anxious), know we have a resource in God, who has brought us this far. It may look pretty in nine months, but if we're not speaking it won't *be* pretty.

ANNIE: When I think of the step we're taking, I hear what you're saying. People are at different places. We have to be sensitive that there are these different levels of response. . . . [We need to] reach out [to them and make sure they're with us].

MARY: If they're in a different place, it doesn't mean they're not supportive—just different.

CONNIE: This conversation reminds me: I was looking at an inchworm in the garden yesterday, inching along. There's a contraction, then it moves. It is goal-oriented.

MARY: We have to move in an undulating motion—

WOODY: —with the whole body coming together.

MARY: The vestry has said we must keep coming back, keep operating as a church, make sure everybody is together. Not that other things *stop*, but this is the lens for now.

Looking back over this meeting, the research advisory committee compared it to "ordinary times" in individual spiritual guidance:

CELIA: What I'm hearing from them is "We've got so much going on"—remember that vision Mary had about people fixing up the church? Well, they're doing it! There's all this money-raising, hammering, whatever. I sense that their concern is "Let's just make sure that our being is all right while we're doing all this stuff." That sounds on target to me. They don't need anything else to do right now!

JERRY: As you well know, there's a lot of individual spiritual direction that goes on where there's no problem to be solved, there's no great insight or experience to be looked at, nothing to be interpreted—it's just a kind of check-in opportunity to reflect on "How's it going with your soul?" And the response is "Fine."

CELIA: That's my sense of it.

TILDEN: It's a kind of confident spirituality. It's sufficient: people know who God is for them and what they're doing together. Right now it's all they have the capacity, willingness, space for. So there you are as temperature taker: "Well, how are you being with this doing?"

Jerry: So often in church groups, the emphasis is on the outcome. With discernment, it is the process that is everything. You could end one of these processes without coming to any plan, but in the process, sharing, prayerfulness, [everything that's needed] could all be there.

LEARNING FROM THE DISCERNMENT STORIES

You may already have some initial leadings about what your church might find useful from the stories. Perhaps it will help to review some of the main points in this chapter on discernment.

We began and ended with the primacy of being and doing as an integrated whole. Before discernment is deciding to do anything, it is being available to God. We can't know we've made the right decision; we can only trust the living Spirit already at work in us. What's happening in us is more important than any outcome.

* * * * *

The Church . . . needs to be aware of its particular institutional responsibility and opportunity for fostering an authentic and corporate rhythm of life that nourishes this "root of inner wisdom" and help it connect with compassionate action. At this root of wisdom is a trust that life is a gift before it is a work; that besides a task, life is given an end-in-itself love by its Lover, a Gospel-Good News that frees us to *allow* dependent/nourishment/appreciation time, without fear that we will collapse into nothingness when we no longer "produce" our own identity and the world's.

   With such trust, we can afford to "rest" in appreciation of the mysterious *givenness* of our most basic identity ("I have called you by name, you are mine." Isa. 43:1).

—Tilden Edwards, *Spiritual Friend*[1]

* * * * *

As you plan ways for corporate discernment, look for whole-person ways—ways that help us be immediately present, including *all* of us—including our unconscious, our imaginations, and practices—not just our heads. As we seek wholeness, let us be whole in our way of seeking. And we have to find the ways that are right for our unique spiritual community, just as St. Patrick's and all the other churches sought to do.

   You may wish to ponder the different decisions about leadership these churches made—and others are possible. There were advantages to the collegial team leadership at Ascension, Lexington Park, where the teamwork provided openings for some possible shifts in leadership as the discernment continued. Remember the possibilities inherent in St. Peter's example of an in-the-moment shift of leadership, when the Mary-Martha story was suggested. Think of how my leading allowed Betty to "play with the people" of St. Patrick's. Jim Holmes's leadership of the main part of the process seemed a good way to make sure that our work would be grounded in the culture of St. Thomas' Parish. You may want to consider the advantages of an outside spiritual companion.

Discerning our gifts may be a good way to start, and interviews can help us surface a congregation's gifts. Gifts are what we've already been given, and may form the core of our calling. And focusing on our gifts is likely to provide us with positive energy—as it did for St. Patrick's, a very discouraged, exhausted church.

Perhaps you will want to think of some graphic way of helping your people look at your church as a person-on-a-journey. You may want to consider using some form of African Bible Study, adapting it as seems right for your parish and people. Or follow Walter Wink to a meeting with the angel of your church.

Let us own and honor our congregation's stories and look for signs of God's presence in them. Whatever plan you make, keep listening. Like Steve and the people at St. Peter's, stay open to surprises that may reflect the leading of the Spirit.

Above all, encourage people to keep praying for each other and the parish. This is what it's all about—the prayer of the people and pastor, and that prayer takes many forms. Betty asked God, "What are you saying to me about these people?" and wrote down the answers that came. Mary hears that "more is going on than you know," and carries her parishioners with her on her daily rounds on Post-It Notes. Steve is aware that his "Our Father" at the end of the day is a "corporate prayer."

You and your people have your own way of asking.

O God, our great Companion, lead us ever more deeply into
the mystery of your life and ours.
You might want to ask right now—alone or together.

Part III

Uncovering Your Church's Hidden Spirit

Research Learnings
That May Offer
Practical Help to Churches

This book is not an abstract treatise on the spiritual development of congregations, nor is it a workbook with six simple steps. If what we have been saying is on target, every church needs to notice how it develops its spiritual life and discern how to follow, adjust, and enlarge those ways in a manner that is right *for that unique congregation.*

At the same time, this book does tell about some ways used to understand and invite the spiritual life of five churches over a two-year period. I can tell you what we did (and we did everything with many variations—one size does not seem to fit more than one church), and report what seemed helpful and what didn't. You can use our experience if it fits, and design your own alternatives where that seems best, possibly guided by some hints you picked up in this book.

CHAPTER 10

How We Discovered
the Lay Spiritual Leaders

Interviews of congregational spiritual leaders are a good way to under-stand your church's corporate spirituality and to reveal your church's gifts, and you might want to consider conducting them. Here are some things we learned about beginning that process.

To find the laypeople to interview, we created a questionnaire titled "Who should be interviewed for this project? We want your nominations," which every church put in its worship bulletin.

Patrick Henry, of the Institute for Ecumenical and Cultural Research in Collegeville, Minnesota, made the suggestion early: "One of the most intriguing ways to go about it would be to ask them to list three or four people they think you should interview and then say why. Spiritual maturity becomes something embodied. Talk to the few who are on everybody's list." I agreed instantly: "A questionnaire to the congregation would give us a *congregational* slant on perceptions about spirituality."

I moved ahead with this plan, circulated a draft of possible questions to the advisory committee for feedback, and designed a church-bulletin-sized questionnaire. Clergy were very willing to put it in the Sunday bulletin, col-lect responses, and adjust the list of most-frequently-named "sages" so that it didn't include all men, or all newcomers, for example, but was reasonably balanced. Many parishioners responded. This way of finding the right people to interview had the important effect of *identifying the lay spiritual lead-ers of the congregation.* The project evaluation indicates how empower-ing this method was for many of those chosen. Here is the bulletin insert:

Churches Nourishing a Spirituality for the World

Who should be interviewed for this project?
We want your nominations.

Among your fellow parishioners,

- To whom would you turn for help in going deeper in your spiritual life?
- Who would you want to pray for you?
- Who especially contributes to the spiritual life of this congregation?
- Who do you think lets their spirituality carry over into all aspects of their life?
- Who contributes to the life of our parish by challenging our assumptions about spiritual life?
- Who might be on the margins of this parish because of the way most people think?

Please feel free to nominate yourself.

Here are my nominations of people in this parish who should be interviewed for the project:

_____
_____
_____
_____
_____

In my view, a spiritually mature person is

_____

_____

_____

CHAPTER 11

Interviews Using the Ware
Questionnaire

We discovered several important reasons for using Corinne Ware's *Discover Your Spiritual Type*[1] as a "diving board" into the interviews. Previous studies had revealed how difficult it often is for people to talk about their spiritual lives, for which they often lack words, and so it seemed a good idea to provide some provisional language and concepts. I had used this questionnaire in retreats with other churches, and had been impressed with the way it includes everyone in the group, with all its diversity. Sometimes this point seemed especially significant for "head" spirituality types, who often don't *think* of themselves as "spiritual"; they are likely to assume that spirituality is "something other people do."

The questionnaire also suggests a belief that we are one body made up of many members who contribute different strengths.

I sent the following letter to interviewees surfaced by the questionnaire and the clergy:

■■■■■■■■■■■■■■■■■■■■■■■■■■■■■■■

Dear _____ :

What is Spirituality? Many people are talking about spirituality today, and the word is being used in lots of different ways. St. Augustine helps me understand this word "spiritual." "Thou hast made us for Thyself, and our hearts are restless until they find their rest in Thee," and draw all that we are in touch with and all those who are part of our lives to God.

For me, "spiritual" means anything that speaks about that restlessness of our hearts, our yearning for or sense of connection with God, and, for us in this project, especially as we know it within the communion of our parish life.

"Discover Your Spiritual Type"—A Helpful Tool. This simple series of questions, designed by Corinne Ware (a seminary professor and member of our research advisory committee) gives us a way to think and talk about how we are the same as others, how we differ, and how we might enrich our own and each other's spiritual growth. Our different ways of being spiritual don't have to separate us: we can come together into a whole that's richer because of our differences. We all need each other. Of course all type theories have their limitations, but you, like many others, may find that this test gives you new insights about your own spiritual life and that of your church.

To get started. Look at the circle diagrams with two intersecting lines on page 53 of Ware's book *Discover Your Spiritual Type*—the section titled "The Spirituality Wheel." [*Note to reader*: Look back at page 4 for a similar diagram.] As you may remember, the vertical line indicates *how we go about knowing:* through our rational minds, with our heads; or with our hearts, our feelings. The horizontal line indicates *how we conceptualize God*—in an emptying ("apophatic") way, knowing God as mystery, or in an imaging ("kataphatic") way, seeing God as revealed, knowable. Spiritual wholeness means including all parts of the circle, even if that means just appreciating the others.

The *four quadrants* identify four types of spirituality. Here is a brief introduction ("Four Spiritual Types," chapter 3 in Ware's book, will give you a more complete picture):

Type 1, *a head spirituality.* God is known with the mind and seen as revealed. Those whose spirituality falls in this quadrant want to make sense of their experience. It's particularly important to them that thought and belief be congruent. They join study groups, listen eagerly to sermons, like to discuss theology. With all their strengths, if Type 1 people get too one-sided, they can get into a "head trip"—a dry rationalism. To enrich their experience they need to explore the opposite quadrant, Type 3, emphasizing introspection and silence. (For each type, the quadrant diagonally across the circle may offer hints for a future stage of spiritual growth.)

Type 2, *a heart spirituality.* Those with this more devotional spirituality are "all heart." As with Type 1, God is revealed, Scripture is central—but here spirituality is affective, heart-centered. These people seek personal renewal and a holy life, and it's exciting to them to share their experience. They offer warmth of feeling, energy, freedom of expression. When too one-sided, they become "pietistic," too exclusive—"us against the world." Their spirituality is enriched as they begin to value other ways of being faithful.

Type 3, *a mystic spirituality.* These folk are also affective, feeling types, but they are more interested in hearing from God than in speaking to God. These contemplative, introspective, intuitive spiritual journeyers are looking for renewal of the inner life, union with the holy. The inner world is as real to them as the exterior world, and a simple life may help quiet distractions. Seeking renewal of the inner life, they may find they don't fit in Western Protestantism. Type 3's way of being too one-sided is "quietism," an exaggerated retreat from interaction with the world. They need to alternate retreat time with involvement.

Type 4, *a kingdom spirituality.* This smallest group combines the mystic experience with an intellectual way of knowing. These active visionaries aim to obey God. Single-minded crusaders, they are inclined to be assertive, even aggressive in their zeal to establish their vision of the world as kingdom of God on earth. They may say, "My work and my prayer are one." You'd find Type 4s in the Peace Corps and in the freedom marches. Their way of being too one-sided is "moralism"—an unrelenting tunnel vision. They make us uncomfortable, but we admire their willingness to make a difference. The 4s need to learn that they don't have to be driven to be faithful.

Now take the test for yourself and your church (about 15 minutes), following the instructions on page 49 of Ware's book, and continuing with the questions on page 50. You can then read more about your type on pages 37ff.

You might want to think, write in a journal, or talk with someone else about these questions:

- What did you find out about yourself that you didn't know?
- What strengths does the test say you have?
- Does your type's way of being "one-sided" fit your experience? In what ways?
- Where is your "growing edge"—your opposite quadrant?
- How is your spirituality the same as, or different from, that of your church?

Please bring your completed "wheels" on page 53 of Ware's book to the interview, and we'll move on from there. I'm looking forward to it!

Blessings,

Celia Allison Hahn

■■■■■■■■■■■■■■■■■■■■■■■■■■■■■■■■

If you decide to use the Ware Instrument, here are some cautions to consider. All such instruments involve cost as well as promise, in that they can make matters appear deceptively simple. This cost is mitigated in this instrument in that it is not a forced-choice questionnaire, and leaves people free to answer in a way that may bring forth a complex, personally tailored result. While talking to the interviewee, the interviewer needs to set the categories in mental brackets and listen prayerfully.

You don't know a congregation through categories any more than you know a person through knowing their Myers-Briggs type (another personality categorizing scheme). All you really have is something like a ZIP code: many different people live in each one. I encountered some objections to the inventory on the part of interviewees. People at Ascension (Silver Spring) and St. Thomas' Parish sometimes objected to the whole idea of categorizing people. I always learned something important about the church when people did object, and the objections often led to fruitful observations. In those two churches, people were especially eager to focus on their reality that the separating power of differences had been *overcome*; they opposed the whole idea of suggesting categories that they feared might divide people. This was useful information for me, and I do not believe these objections offset the value of the instrument in the project.

In my interviews I noticed that a special problem emerged with Quadrant 4. Quite a few people I interviewed tested as Quadrant 4, but in my interviewing experience head-apophatic types don't necessarily express their faith in the form of social action, nor are social activists necessarily head-apophatic types. I learned to put this type description in parentheses, as it were, to acknowledge to the interviewee what I was doing, where appropriate, and to look for the spiritual place where the person seemed to be, regardless of the book description.

Incidentally, I like John Ackerman's simple headings for the quadrants—thinking, feeling, being, and doing—and would have found them useful in interviewing.

In addition to the costs and cautions, many promises are inherent in the use of this instrument. As a result of the Ware Inventory, all interviewees had a rather clear sense of where their church was on the instrument, and therefore were helped in considering what potential directions for spiritual growth seemed right. I found also that the test revealed or clarified type differences or similarities between the clergy and laity in a congregation, an observation that could be followed up with benefit to illuminate the church's life. The book *Discover Your Spiritual Type* also offers many suggestions for congregational use of the instrument.

CHAPTER 12

Interviewing:
A Way to Discover a Church's Gifts

Interviews can help you uncover a church's corporate spirituality and gifts. I suggest you consider interviewing as part of your discernment. Here we take a look at the interview questions carefully worked out in consultation with the research advisory committee, learnings about how to interview, and the interview process, including some of its inherent spiritual possibilities.

THE INTERVIEW QUESTIONS

All agreed that the questions "worked," and again it was demonstrated that one can ask laypeople questions like "Do you have any sense of where God might be leading this church?" and get very perceptive answers. I think we have to keep learning this over the decades because interviewing laypeople in this way is profoundly countercultural: professionals often don't *expect* laity to be able to respond in any meaningful way to such a question.

Your church might not want to conduct such long interviews (these took up to one-and-a-half hours each and involved considerable transcription costs). I've guessed at a few questions that might be especially helpful to include in a simpler, shorter interview (these are marked with an asterisk). But in this, as in all such matters, be guided by your own discernment.

Questions for Interviews with Parishioners

In interviewing, recognize that "spiritual" is often not part of people's working vocabulary. In your conversations vary your language, as appropriate, using words like "connected," "centered," "at home," etc. ("I" questions focus on individual experience, "C" questions on the congregation.)

I-1. * In what ways do you find yourself more readily sensing/experiencing God?
[Touch back to Ware instrument]

I-2. What changes have you noticed in your relationship with God over the years?
[You may want to use the Ware instrument where it fits—e.g., people sometimes find that during their lives they shift from predominantly head spirituality to mystic, or make some other kind of shift diagonally across the circle diagram.]
Have you noticed yourself concentrating more in one area?
* Has this made a difference in your daily life and work?

I-3. * How have the parish, the clergy influenced your spiritual journey?

I-4. Tell me about a group or a person who made a difference for your spiritual life. What happened?

I-5. How long have you been coming to this church?
(To newcomers): What drew you to this parish? What helped you become a part of it?
(To old-timers): What keeps you here in this parish?

I-6. Has your being male or female influenced your relationship with God in any way you are aware of?

I-7. * Do you have any sense of where God may be leading you now in your life?

I-8. * Given that sense of movement, what do you sense you need most to nurture your spiritual life now?

C-1.* What role might your parish play in that spiritual nurturing? Your clergy?

And now let's continue, moving on from your own individual experience, and concentrate a bit more on the spirituality of the congregation as you perceived it through the Ware instrument.

C-2.* How did your parish get the focus it has?
What spiritual practices have been used to help you get here?
How are the areas we focus on less (intellectual, devotional, mystical, or social action) included as part of the whole picture in this parish?

C-3.* Do you have any sense that God seems to be leading your congregation in a particular direction?

Any sense that God seems to be leading your congregation toward some way of holding all these ways of being spiritual together?

[*Note about Question I-6*: I soon learned that this was not a useful question in this day and age. People almost invariably denied that there were differences between men and women, and the question elicited no useful responses from lay respondents, and few from clergy.]

Questions for Interviews with Clergy

CL-1. * In what ways do you find yourself more readily knowing/sensing/experiencing God? [Touch back to Ware instrument.]

CL-2. * What changes have you noticed in your relationship with God over the years? Have you noticed yourself concentrating more in one area? [You may want to use the Ware instrument where it fits—for example, people sometimes find that during their lives they shift from predominantly head spirituality to mystic, or make other kinds of shifts diagonally across the circle diagram.]

CL-3. Has your being male or female influenced your relationship with God in any way you are aware of? [This question elicited somewhat more response from clergy than laity.]

CL-4. * As you reflect on your response to the Ware instrument, what can you tell me about the connections between your relationship with God and your spiritual leadership in the congregation?

CL-5. * What influence has this congregation had on your spiritual growth?

CL-6. Given your spiritual focus, do your relationships with parishioners support you? Threaten you? Or . . . ?

CL-7. * Do you have any sense that God seems to be leading your congregation in a particular direction or to some particular integration of the four main strengths?

Offer clergy interviewees a general sense of where the lay interviewees in their parish seem to be. Then ask:

CL-8. What is your sense of the web of relationships between you and parishioners like these?

CL-9.   What does this say about your role in this parish, and your feelings
         about that role? Does it make a difference?

[*Note*: You may be wondering, "What if we, in our church, are not planning
to get anybody else to work with us on the interviews?" If there seems no
good way to arrange for interviews with clergy or lay leaders, here is a
substitute idea: a pastor and lay participants might go through these questions and prayerfully write responses in to them, then compare notes with
the others participating. This substitute will not have the value of an actual
interview (the two-person encounter holds a special power), but it could be
useful in encouraging prayerful thought about these questions, and it would
provide some thoughtful preparation for discerning the church's gifts.]

The Process of the Interview

Let's back off from the questions themselves now, and think about the
process of the interview. Here we may be guided along the way by Henri
Nouwen's thoughts about hospitality, for interviewing at its best is a form of
hospitality. "Our most important question . . . is not, 'What to say or to do?'
but, 'How to develop enough inner space where the story can be received?'"[1]
        Preparing to allow the inner space to receive the unique stories of
these people, I try to center myself in my hope and intention to be open to
God, and open to this person. Please join me now, as we get ready to spend
a little time with some interviewees from the churches in the project.

Take a deep breath, right down to your middle.

As you breathe out, let all tension flow out.

Sitting aware on the edge of mystery,
With God as your companion,
Center yourself as you prepare to open yourself
to some ordinarily hidden places
in the lives of those we are about to meet.

LISTENING TO THE UNIQUE STORIES

Here are some segments of three interviews. Open yourself to simply meeting these three people. Don't feel you have to do anything beyond just being present to them. Just listen along with me to what they are revealing about themselves, their spiritual lives, and their communities.

Family Split

CELIA: So, what has the experience been like for you and this church to have a lot of people walk out because of their strong feelings about that [the ordination of gay clergy]?

M: Do you know what it's like to have a death in your immediate family? I would cry when I would come.

CELIA: So it's just been enormously painful to see the family split apart . . . . What about the life of this church as you have served it since that very hard time? How do you think things are going?

M: I think it's back on track. . . . It took a while, but once again there were others who said, "We don't have any place else to go [*whispered*]. This is my church and I'm staying, so—

CELIA: So you think the church has been able to move on from that time?

M: I think so.

CELIA: Tell me a little more.

[*M elaborates.*]

CELIA: It sounds like some of this has been troubling to you.

M: It has.

CELIA: Can you tell me a little bit about that?

M: Well, I have been less than pleased with ordination of practicing homosexuals.

CELIA: Mmm-hmm.

M: That was the thing that just about tore this church apart, and many people left, as you know.

CELIA: Right.

M: And I teetered on the brink.

CELIA: Because you really didn't agree with that.

M: I didn't agree with that.

A Safe Place for the "Special Children"

CELIA: So I'm glad you had a chance to look a little bit at the instrument. Did you get a chance to put some marks in the circles? Good.

D: Easier for me to do on myself than on the congregation.

CELIA: Well, I would think it would be. So how did it come out with your own circle?

D: I am mostly a 1[on the Ware test]. But I have parts of 2 and 4. The least I have is 3. But I had some in each one. I have a child who is—I have two children who are special but one for whom being a 1, which I suppose I was raised as, does not work. So that, if I remember correctly, I have a great many 2s because when you have a child who is retarded and who is clearly spiritual, there are a lot of things that go away, that no longer make any sense.

CELIA: Approaching this with the heart seems to be brought out by the special child.

D: Uh, a lot of things happen when you have children who don't fit the norm. . . . I don't know why I'm crying because it [experiencing the church as a family] is a nice thing, but—

CELIA: You must need a family a lot with all these challenges and to think that it's here and kids can come and it's a safe place if they wander—

D: It's a place that stretches them too. . . . I would say that it's a family that is kind of leading by example and that more than anything I think has made it fun but growing. . . . So there we are. So that's my family. . . .

CELIA: It makes a lot of sense.

D: Sorry for the tears.

CELIA: I don't think there's any need to be sorry. A lot of people cry during these interviews.

D: Oh, do they?

CELIA: This seems to happen with a fair number of people because we don't sit and talk about things like this very often and I think it touches a deep place in our lives, and it moves us. . . . Can you tell me about a group or a person who has made a difference for your spiritual life? Maybe you have just done that.

God as Mystery

E: I don't think I could speak for the congregation very much.

CELIA: That's all right. Let's start with you.

E: I imagine that it would be possible, but I don't feel that I'm qualified to speak for—

CELIA: Well, all we can do is guess. So if you felt like guessing, fine. And if you didn't, let's just talk about you. So can you give me some idea of how that came out for you?

E: OK, "God is mystery and can be grasped for, but not completely known." *That is me.*

CELIA: That's really important to you.

E: I—it's all a mystery, and I don't believe I'm supposed to figure [it] out. I don't think that's for us to decide.

CELIA: So you're very comfortable with the idea of God as mystery.

E: Yup.

CELIA: And that was the main thing that you said yes to, a big yes to.

E: Yes. Because I'm not sure I could do a thing about it if I knew more, and I don't know it, and I don't know how to find out. So I just leave it in God's hands. . . . So as I say, I guess I learned a good bit [from this questionnaire], but up until this came, I'm afraid I hadn't given much of this much thought.

CELIA: That's OK. Part of the purpose of this is to give us some common ways to talk about something that many of us don't talk about very much.

E: You think that's not unusual.

CELIA: No, I don't think that's unusual.

E: I wasn't sure. It certainly is true with me. Definitely. . . . As I say, I really haven't given it a whole lot of thought. I'm just thinking, let me go through this life, and the next one will be all right.

CELIA: Sort of a sense of basic trust.

E: I think so. Yes.

CELIA: That's always been with you—

E: But as far as trying to grasp things, as I say, there's too much mystery to me. And I don't know how; I don't know that I'm supposed to know. I'm not sure that I have to dig into something like that. For me.

CELIA: That's OK. Let it be that way for you.

E: In other words, I just feel secure. And I don't think I would be able to

decide anything definite anyway—I mean, how would I know? That's the way I feel about it this. What may come, will come.
CELIA: So you're comfortable with mystery, and you're comfortable with leaving it in God's hands.

Take a few minutes now to mull over what struck you first about these encounters, and perhaps make a few notes for yourself.

———————————————————————————————

———————————————————————————————

———————————————————————————————

———————————————————————————————

Here are some of my reflections on these excerpts from the interviews. I get a hint of how utterly unique people are when I descend to the realm of the hidden spirit with them—the individual spirit and the corporate soul of the congregation. Many times they are unsure of how to talk about those depths, partly because it is hard, and partly because often nobody has ever asked.

As Nouwen reflects: "[L]istening is an art that must be developed, not a technique that can be applied as a monkey wrench to nuts and bolts. It needs the full and real presence of people to each other. It is indeed one of the highest forms of hospitality."[2]

People's uniqueness, the probable initial strangeness of this kind of conversation, the power people experience in hospitable, full, and real presence—those are some reasons why I believe it's important to let people know they have been heard. One way to do that is to tell them what I heard them say. And it may be important to people to be validated—to hear: "It makes sense that you. . . ." When we have a chance to talk about what's deepest in our hearts—a chance we haven't had much of—it often moves us to tears. If interviewees cry, it may be useful to indicate that this is not uncommon. They don't know that.

During the interview, as I listen, I become aware of parts of the question that this person can speak about in a way no one else could; this makes me want to pursue the path of inquiry by probing for this person's experience and response.

I feel free to spend extra time on questions, or to move through some very quickly (or even, occasionally, to skip a question), depending on the promise of response or lack of it. The questions are an important guide, but you are on a "dig," here, and you'll be exploring at a number of points— some will be dry holes; others will prove promising sites for learning about the spirituality of your congregation and its people.

Here are the same segments of interviews now presented with mirroring ("this is what I heard") or validating ("what you say makes sense to me") responses in *italics*, and with probing questions in SMALL CAPITAL LETTERS. You might want to notice what those responses seem to evoke in the interviewee.

* * * * *

CELIA: SO, WHAT HAS THE EXPERIENCE BEEN LIKE FOR YOU AND THIS CHURCH TO HAVE A LOT OF PEOPLE WALK OUT BECAUSE OF THEIR STRONG FEELINGS ABOUT THAT?

M: Do you know what it's like to have a death in your immediate family? I would cry when I would come.

CELIA: *So it's just been enormously painful to see the family split apart.* . . . WHAT ABOUT THE LIFE OF THIS CHURCH AS YOU HAVE SERVED IT SINCE THAT VERY HARD TIME? HOW DO YOU THINK THINGS ARE GOING?

M: I think it's back on track. . . . It took a while, but once again there were others who said, "We don't have any place else to go" [*whispered*]. This is my church and I'm staying, so—

CELIA: SO YOU THINK THE CHURCH HAS BEEN ABLE TO MOVE ON FROM THAT TIME?

M: I think so.

CELIA: TELL ME A LITTLE MORE.

[*M elaborates.*]

CELIA: *It sounds like some of this has been troubling to you.*

M: It has.

CELIA: CAN YOU TELL ME A LITTLE BIT ABOUT THAT?

M: Well, I have been less than pleased with ordination of practicing homosexuals.

CELIA: *Mmm-hmm.*

M: That was the thing that just about tore this church apart and many people left, as you know.

CELIA: Right.

M: And I teetered on the brink.

CELIA: *Because you really didn't agree with that.*

M: I didn't agree with that.

* * * * *

CELIA: So I'm glad you had a chance to look a little bit at the instrument. Did you get a chance to put some marks in the circles? *Good.*

D: Easier for me to do on myself than on the congregation.

CELIA: *Well, I would think it would be.* So how did it come out with your own circle?

D: I am mostly a 1[on the Ware test]. But I have parts of 2 and 4. The least I have is 3. But I had some in each one. I have a child who is—I have two children who are special, but one for whom being a 1, which I suppose I was raised as, does not work. So that, if I remember correctly, I have a great many 2s because when you have a child who is retarded and who is clearly spiritual, there are a lot of things that go away, that no longer make any sense.

CELIA: *Approaching this with the heart seems to be brought out by the special child.*

D: Uh, a lot of things happen when you have children who don't fit the norm *[pause]*. I don't know why I'm crying because it [experiencing the church as a family] is a nice thing, but—

CELIA: *You must need a family a lot with all these challenges and to think that it's here and kids can come and it's a safe place if they wander—*

D: It's a place that stretches them too. . . . I would say that it's a family that is a kind of a leading by example and that more than anything I think has made it fun but growing. . . . So there we are. So that's my family.

CELIA: *It makes a lot of sense.*

D: Sorry for the tears.

CELIA: I don't think there's any need to be sorry. A lot of people cry during these interviews.

D: Oh, do they?

CELIA: This seems to happen with a fair number of people because we don't sit and talk about things like this very often and I think it touches a deep place in our lives, and it moves us. Can you tell me about a group or a person who has made a difference for your spiritual life? Maybe you have just done that.

* * * * *

E: I don't think I could speak for the congregation very much.

CELIA: *That's all right.* Let's start with you.

E: I imagine that it would be possible but I don't feel that I'm qualified to speak for—

CELIA: Well, all we can do is guess. So if you felt like guessing, fine. And if you didn't, let's just talk about you. So can you give me some idea of how that came out for you?

E: OK, "God is mystery and can be grasped for, but not completely known." *That is me.*

CELIA: *That's really important to you.*

E: I—it's all a mystery, and I don't believe I'm supposed to figure it out. I don't think that's for us to decide.

CELIA: *So you're very comfortable with the idea of God as mystery.*

E: Yup.

CELIA: *And that was the main thing that you said yes to, a big yes to.*

E: Yes. Because I'm not sure I could do a thing about it if I knew more, and I don't know it, and I don't know how to find out. So I just leave it in God's hands. . . . So as I say, I guess I learned a good bit [from this questionnaire], but up until this came, I'm afraid I hadn't given much of this much thought.

CELIA: That's OK. *Part of the purpose of this is to give us some common ways to talk about something that many of us don't talk about very much.*

E: You think that's not unusual.

CELIA: *No, I don't think that's unusual.*

E: I wasn't sure. It certainly is true with me. Definitely. . . . As I say, I really haven't given it a whole lot of thought. I'm just thinking, let me go through this life, and the next one will be all right.

CELIA: *Sort of a sense of basic trust.*

E: I think so. Yes.

CELIA: *That's always been with you....*

[Pause]

E: But as far as trying to grasp things, as I say, there's too much mystery to me. And I don't know how, I don't know that I'm supposed to know. I'm not sure that I have to dig into something like that. For me.

CELIA: *That's OK. Let it be that way for you.*

E: In other words, I just feel secure. And I don't think I would be able to decide anything definite anyway, I mean, how would I know? That's the way I feel about it this. What may come, will come.

CELIA : So you're comfortable with mystery and you're comfortable with leaving it in God's hands.

REFLECTING ON THE PROCESS OF INTERVIEWING

The variety of spiritual styles is amazing; it confirms my impression that people are most unique, most different from one another in the dimension of their spirituality. This realization evokes in me an enormous respect, and a desire to listen in a cherishing way. Sometimes people are inarticulate, yet they communicate the quality of their spiritual life. As Nouwen puts it:

> Why is listening to know through and through such a healing service? Because it makes strangers familiar with the terrain they are traveling through and helps them to discover the way they want to go. Many of us have lost our sensitivity for our own history and experience our life as a capricious series of events over which we have no control. When all our attention is drawn away from ourselves and absorbed by what happens around us, we become strangers to ourselves, people without a story to tell or to follow up.[3]

Most important, *it is possible to become acquainted with vital dimensions of the soul of the congregation through listening to its people.* It's a little like walking around a statue and regarding it from many perspectives. After completing all the interviews, stop, meditate over your notes, and notice what you've learned about the hidden spirit of your congregation. With your colleagues, begin to list your church's gifts, given by God.

* * * * *

Healing means first of all allowing strangers to become sensitive and obedient to their own stories.

—Henri Nouwen[4]

* * * * *

Effect on Interviewees

Let's listen to what some interviewees told us in the evaluation about what interviewing meant to them:

A.   *What has it meant to you*

(1) To be interviewed?
BARBARA: It was very enlightening to me personally to be interviewed because it gave me the chance to think about my beliefs in word form instead of notions in my head.
ANNIE: It made me think about something I take for granted. It helped me place my life at this time in context.

(2) To be chosen as an interviewee?

MARGARET: It was an honor to be chosen, but also a surprise. I would like to be a spiritual person but feel I am not.
KAY: I felt the church wanted the voice of an older member and one who has been here since Ascension started. I'm glad you want input from all age groups.
LYNN: It was heartwarming to be seen as a spiritual person by my fellow parishioners.
CONNIE: An opportunity to tell the story of my church as I see it. Having been a longtime member, I have seen how it has evolved until it is where it is now.
ANNIE: Actually this time of my life has been somewhat difficult, and to be chosen as an interviewee has felt somewhat burdensome. However, it caused me to reflect on things I would have been too busy to think about. I would not have chosen to be an interviewee, but I am grateful I was.

B.   *What parts of the experience were positive for you? In what way?*
ANNIE: The fact that I participated was very positive for me. It brought into focus a dimension of my life that I was neglecting that contributed to everything else being out of focus. The interview with Celia Hahn was a very positive experience. Seeing my thoughts in print was also a positive experience.

C. *Was there anything in this experience that surprised you? Please describe.*

    ANNIE: I was a little surprised at the impact this interview had on my thinking. The fact that I had arrived at incorporating my work into my spiritual life—I had not articulated for myself before.

CHAPTER 13

The Use of Story
in the Discernment Process

S tories from interviewees teach us about our church; corporate stories also help churches discern, because they are an important way to discover God-with-us.

Let's go back to St. Peter's, Poolesville, in the Maryland countryside, and walk a little further alongside the people, setting our own church next to theirs in our minds. Are our people at all like theirs, or are they quite different? Where do our stories intersect? What might we learn from them about "story" that would be useful to us?

In the research advisory committee, we kept coming back to storytelling as a "way"—especially for St. Peter's, probably because its story is 250 years long and therefore so powerful in its life, and also because members' concreteness made for good stories. (In years past the congregation included a lot of people in the building trades.)

As he looked back at St. Peter's 250 years of money shortages, Steve Hayward concluded: "God is central to people's survival—they assume that." And that made us wonder: How might they become ready *to voice this assumption aloud?*

Now, consider the life of your own congregation. What is a basic assumption of your church about God (based on its experience or history)? Is this assumption voiced aloud?

For St. Peter's, concreteness is an important quality of life: these are down-to-earth people who say: "We do hands-on stuff." Respecting that reality provides strong experiential anchors for stories. Pancake breakfasts are a great time to tell stories.

Do you have an equivalent of the "pancake breakfast"—a time just right for storytelling? What might that time be? Or is there an inviting possibility for a story setting?

Service is important at St. Peter's—it is rooted in "our story." "We have been in need"—therefore "We have helped others in need," making contributions to their physical survival (in Central America, for example).

What aspect of your congregational life is especially rooted in your church's story?

In the research advisory committee Chuck Olsen retold the "Story of St. Peter's." Corinne Ware imagined the St. Peter's people hearing the story: "I think they would see it as a drama, whereas they may have thought it was ordinary. But to hear it reframed would make it special."

Chuck elaborated on the possibilities of story: "If you came back with an initiative, that would be resisted, but . . . we may ask, 'What might help them reflect theologically on *events* that are real to them? Tangible stories. How they got their name. The heritage of the land.' We can take where they are and go deeper with it."

Story is a fruitful "way" because, as Jerry put it, "People might disclose in story a lot more than they would in answer to a question like: 'What's going on inside you when you pray?'" The story could be a parable, laid alongside their life.

"The important role of story for this congregation is to provide opportunity for them to name God's presence in their own words," concluded Chuck. "There is a charism in St. Peter's about *being on the edge*, and part of the formation here is to rehearse the story of coming to the edge."

What is your congregation's story? What is the charism that is rooted in your congregation's story?

Chuck continued: Steve made an important comment: that they assume that being God-centered is crucial to their survival. My question is: 'How would you help them articulate that assumption?' You might ask:

"1. How did they let go . . . trust in something beyond themselves?

"2. Name how God was present there.

"3. Then, how did they take hold? What did they do about it? Stories about hands-on mission enterprises—how they are continuing to live out their charism—could prompt more stories." To let go, name how God is present, and then to take hold again—this sequence describes a rich spiritual movement.

How could you frame those three questions for your church?

One simple and fun way of helping people tell stories as a group is to suggest they use "And then . . ." or "but before that" as the connecting links for the contributions each person makes. "Let it come naturally, like popcorn," said Chuck, "with short additions, and encourage them to use 'we' rather than 'I.'"

He suggested to parishioners that St. Peter's "tell the story of the last discernment meeting so that they develop corporate memory over it. Then you could use the Mary-Martha story in a different way. What if they would select a story from their experience as a church and then invite the participants to self-select into two groups? Tell the story twice—first from the perspective of Martha and then from the perspective of Mary."

How could you adapt these story-telling ideas for your own discernment process?

Awareness of our story can build powerfully over time. It makes a difference when people get in the habit of asking, "What has God been doing since we last met?" When tough stories come along, these churches have practiced and established a habit of storytelling. The cumulative impact of being a storytelling congregation is the clear sense of being on a journey.

This dialogue between St. Peter's Church and your church, along with the suggestions for prayer scattered through this book, might be a prototype for how you might use this book as a guide for your church's spiritual deepening. If you are working with a discernment group in your own church, you might choose sections of this book that seem to "speak to your condition," and meditate or engage in dialogue with them in your own way.

CHAPTER 14

Further Dimensions
of the Discernment Process

We set forth a basic background for discernment in part II, with examples of several kinds of discernment meetings. Now we turn to some specific learnings from the study to suggest how you might move forward from that background, tailoring the process to your church as you listen for God's call. In the project churches the discernment group was composed of the pastor and the interviewees. In some churches, other parish leaders were added (at St. Peter's, for instance, the members of the vestry's "spiritual life committee"). These groups then engaged in the kinds of discernment meetings you read about in part II.

We've been talking about prayer (and, I hope, praying) throughout the book. Here are some additional thoughts.

A. PRAYER: BACKGROUND AND FOREGROUND OF THE PROCESS

I prayed for the churches regularly throughout the process (and I still pray for them). I made up a little bidding (inviting) prayer for myself to help me focus on each church, and shared that with the people in the discernment groups. (A strong part of my agenda in telling them about this was to encourage *them* to pray.) We ended every discernment meeting by asking people to keep this process and the life of their church in their prayers.

When I met with the clergy, we usually began with silence for "centering." Clergy often shared their prayers about the process with me, as you will have noticed in the discernment section.

Scripture that seemed to speak to the churches' condition often rose out of silences in the research advisory committee's meetings. And prayer was there between meetings as well, as you can see by this e-mail message from Richard Chiola: "At prayer this morning I wondered how you were doing and got a response that exactly matched your fax, which I just read. I am so pleased that the questions we worked on and using Ware for an introduction worked as I had hoped. Both you and the respondents felt that spiritual direction was happening."

And you are part of this network of prayer. Throughout this book, I have tried to offer suggestions to you about how to "pray over" this process as you go through it. And of course you will find the ways that are right for you. You will think of other opportunities for prayer, so that in every way this book becomes a "prayer book," not just a "workbook" in which you might expect to follow the recipes and get the result you want.

B. When to Begin the Discernment Process

It is important to think about how your first discernment meeting (like those described in part II) might fit into a larger picture, an ongoing process. Choose a time for this discernment process when you can have continuity, not a time when you will be interrupted by summer and busy high points in the church year. Work out with the participants what the best time frame is for your church. Connie noted correctly in her evaluation that there was "too much lapse of time" between the steps in the process, which caused us to lose momentum.

Here's another kind of reflection about timing from Mary Sulerud's evaluation: "Assess the overall congregational development needs of the congregation first. If there are huge administrative and stewardship discernments to be made, and there were in our case, approach this experience ready as the ordained leader to do a lot of 'bridgework' about helping people see that conversations about spirituality are very pragmatic!"

And invite commitment to a patient, prayerful process.

C. Who Should Be Involved in the Discernment Process?

Here are some of our learnings from the project. The clergy and I jointly planned whom we ought to include in the meetings, and came up with different answers in different churches. Looking back, I conclude that beginning with a meeting including rector and interviewees only, as we did at

Ascension, Silver Spring, seemed the best way to start. These people have been surfaced as the lay spiritual leaders of the congregation; they have a shared (though individual) experience in the interviews and a beginning sense of themselves as a group. At the other churches, representatives of appropriate parish organizations were included, which seemed to be a reasonable way to proceed at the time. But the groups with newly added representatives seemed to lack the "glue" experienced in a group made up of interviewees only. We did not take enough time and care to bring the new people on board, so that it sometimes proved difficult to incorporate these new parishioners in the discernment process. If the discerning were not confined to a two-year action research project, but were ongoing, it would be important to plan with the pastor how to proceed, enlarging the group gradually with care to bring new people on board so as not to lose the identity, shared experience, and momentum of the initial discernment group. Then you would plan ways to move out in broader and broader ripples, so that eventually a significant part of the congregation would be involved in the discernment process. (You will be able to do *more* than we could, and we invite your story to extend the learnings of this project for churches. See the questions at the end of the book.)

D. THE POWER OF IDEAS FROM ADVISORS

If you, as either in-parish or outside facilitator of the discernment process, work with a group of advisors, or companions in a peer group, you will probably find that your advisors can be very helpful to you. You may also find that they often don't seem to quite "get it" about the congregation you're describing. That's bound to be so, because every congregation is unique and full of mystery: you can't fully describe it. In our conversations about the congregations, I think the research advisory committee got sick of hearing me respond: "Well, it isn't quite like that there." They were experts in the field and often brilliant at developing conceptual schemes, many of which were helpful—you've been reading about them. But because they didn't know the congregations firsthand, the brilliant concepts sometimes didn't seem to touch the ground. I would suggest listening to others' ideas prayerfully, but being very discerning about which of their ideas really fit, even if your advisors know more about congregational studies or discernment than you do. Stay conscious and respectful of the mystery of the congregation's unique spirit.

And regard the congregation and its leaders with great sensitivity to their uniqueness and to their passionate and dedicated attachment to the life of their church. If you have thoughts from outside advisors, discern with great care what might be truly useful to this pastor and these lay members at this time. I did share with the clergy a major part of the research advisory committee's reflections on their church. In a couple of cases this was seen as very helpful. Mary Sulerud wrote in her evaluation, "These were really challenging, insightful, juicy reflections—certainly gave me a lot to pray about." In two churches the committee reflections were seen as very helpful; in one the response was mixed. (Steve Hayward added, "We found the comments to be a little too academic and not focused enough.") In one church the response was more negative than positive, and in another sharing the reflections proved extremely unhelpful. So I urge your careful sensitivity to the power of such ideas from others.

CHAPTER 15

The Role of Spiritual Companion

Clarity about the role of "spiritual companion" to these churches rose out of the two years' work with the congregations and surprised me. Since surprises are always worth careful attention, I'd like first to tell the story of that unexpected learning, then enrich my picture with the reflections and thoughts of my advisory colleagues in the project, and finally pay specific attention to some ways this role might be relevant to you in uncovering your church's hidden spirit—as well as some alternative ways to proceed in case it doesn't seem relevant.

The role of spiritual companion has been used by others in ways broader than individual spiritual direction. I introduced a *Congregations* article by Denise Woods about a ministry with the city of Pasadena, California, in these words: "Spiritual directors seek to be present to God and present to the person who sits before them. As I have begun to practice this kind of presence, I keep being struck by the thought that this is a basic discipline and grace of the Christian way that is relevant far beyond the specific practice of spiritual direction. Listen to Denise Wood describe the ministry to which All Saints Church called her out into the city of Pasadena: 'I had no hidden agenda of my own for these conversations. I wanted to learn, to be taught, to listen.' As she became a mentor for others who joined her in this listening ministry, she concluded, 'It could be said that the parishioners involved in this enterprise were being *present to "what is" in the community and being present to God.'*"[1] Here is an example of the role of spiritual companion to an "other" that is corporate, not individual.

QUALITIES OF THE COMPANION ROLE

Let's look at some of the characteristics of that role of presence as it emerged in the congregational spirituality research. First, spiritual companionship *has more to do with presence than directing.* It's about being before it's about doing. During one research advisory committee meeting, I reported a surprise: "What you're saying makes me realize that a transition is going on in me. We write proposals and say we're going to do *this* and *this*—but the project is changing, being transformed, all the time as we learn. I'm almost embarrassed to hand out that early article about the project anymore, because it doesn't describe where we are now. And I think the whole idea of churches 'taking a next step' I would now bracket, because just as I'm learning that their *present* is about 'being' before 'doing,' I think their *future* is about 'being' flowing into 'doing' too. In the African Bible study, we've used the question, 'What does God call us to do or be?' I would now word that: 'What is God calling us to be, and perhaps do?'"

The role of spiritual companion is a *listening* role. Martha's sister Mary does "the thing most needful"—listening. This means, in the present context too, a receptive, not an active role, *receiving the reality of the congregation* rather than attempting to "direct" it (just as in individual spiritual companionship or direction, the role has been described as "listener, reflector, asker of questions, fellow explorer" much more than effortfulness, or seeking to influence).[2]

A spiritual companion is *like a midwife.* I am aware of trying to be present for people and do what seems useful to support them as they carry out their process. While they do their Bible study in meetings, I pray for them, and this feels very much like midwifery. Margaret Guenther elaborates the metaphor: Unlike the doctor, the midwife "has time." She waits, while "we are not comfortable with waiting. We see it as wasted time and try to avoid it, or at least fill it with trivial busyness. We value action for its own sake. . . . It is hard to trust in the slow work of God . . . the spiritual director does well to emulate the midwife's restraint. . . . She knows when she can assist and interpret and when she should merely be present. She intervenes only when necessary and helpful."[3]

The spiritual companion *walks alongside.* In the role of spiritual companion I really do see myself as walking alongside a person or a church. It's not that the role is devoid of authority, but I don't go in expecting that I'm going to tell people what to do. In her book *Connecting to God*, Corinne

Ware speaks of those "whose task is to accompany, not persuade. . . . Persuasion is God's business. Being 'a friend alongside' is ours"[4] (cf. Matthew 23:8: "[Y]ou are not to be called rabbi, for you have one teacher, and you are all students"). And here I, for one, want to set firmly aside the traditional term "director," which seems to me not only inaccurate but counterproductive at *least* in all churches that have no tradition of this role, and probably in *all churches* except perhaps those that maintain a tradition of directive spiritual mentoring (conservative evangelicals and conservative Roman Catholics).

In working with churches, "walking alongside" implies *a collaborative stance* on the part of the companion. It implies encouraging parishioners' ownership, and that means adopting *a variety of roles*. Lead the meeting so that Betty can "play with the people" (she needs to hear: "You have no task now in this meeting," and her people need her playfully alongside them). Be glad that Jim is leading, so as to keep the St. Thomas' flavor. With the folk at Ascension, Lexington Park, be willing, initially, to take the initiative as they expect, then give it back to them. Encourage their ownership, where needed: for example, when you hear them say "You do it" or "The advisory committee will do it." In sum, the role of spiritually companioning parishes is not, in my experience, fundamentally different from walking alongside individual people.

So the role and authority of the spiritual companion to a congregation, as it has emerged in my work, is to seek to be present to God and be present to "what is" in this community, to be present rather than directing, to listen for the hidden spirit of the congregation. The spiritual companion, like a midwife, is one who walks "alongside," collaborating.

JOINING MYSTERY AND EXPERIENCE

The *purpose* of the spiritual companion's role is hinted at in texts like these: "In Him all things hold together" (Col. 1:17); "God . . . has given us the ministry of reconciliation" (2 Cor. 5:18); and "reuniting the separated," to quote theologian Paul Tillich. That purpose inspires my passion about reuniting "spirituality" and "congregations." Here is a picture of how the "holding together," the "reconciliation," the "reuniting of the separated" may be helped to come about: Imagine an hourglass, with one globe representing mystery and the other representing our experience (it doesn't matter which end is "up"), and the narrow connecting place, where there might be a flowing between them, representing symbol (biblical material, liturgy, etc.). We yearn for our experience to be in conscious touch with mystery. An important way that happens is through symbol. In the stories of spiritual companioning in congregations you have been reading, symbol often takes the form of scriptural words that seem as though they might open the way to this reuniting for us. The hope for reuniting that we glimpse in these words might be sparked, for example, when the folk at St. Thomas' realize it was Thomas who said, "How shall we know the way?" or because we at St. Patrick's, too, hope to get up and walk. The parish group and I then explored the symbolic language in the way this part of the Christian family does it (that is, a "Thomassy" way).

Finally I have to note that any spiritual companioning is a relationship of great mutuality, in which it's not very clear who is giving what to whom—if anything. Anyone who accompanies another person or community in this way receives gifts and discoveries. Richard Chiola added, "If you want a theological term for that, it's *perichoresis*—"dancing" or "indwelling." In the great dance it's not clear who's leading, because we're giving over to one another.

In summary, the role of spiritual companion is a listening role, pointed to by the metaphors of "midwife" and one who "walks alongside." In seeking to collaborate with parish leaders, the spiritual companion adopts a variety of roles, as needed, always respectful of the people's leadership of their church, receiving as well as giving, and joins them in seeking the symbols that might show the connection between our experience and the transcendent mystery.

ADVISORS DESCRIBE COMPANIONING

As the role of spiritual companion took shape in the work with the churches, and I described the living out of this role to my colleagues in the research advisory committee, they responded, contributing their own thoughts:

Corinne Ware commented:

One of the new learnings for me has been the idea that not only can individuals engage in spiritual direction, but churches can benefit from a guide in leading the congregation toward a more aware and hopefully deeper spiritual life. The whole concept of a spirituality consultant, if one may use such a term, is exciting to me. I'm seeing that one of the important uses of a book that may come out of this project is to present to the reader a model for this congregational companionship . . . . We have talked about the importance of just the *presence* of somebody, not that you have a goal that has a certain look to it, but just being present to ask the questions, and I thought about the illustration that so many are using from quantum physics, that *the observer affects the observed* by simply being the observer.

Robert Martin spoke often of "*a ministry of attentiveness* . . . . A participant observer is a ministry that catalyzes what is already going on but makes it more explicit, more intentional, and therefore intensifies what is already going on."

Richard Chiola spoke about "being attentive to the very effect you are having by asking the questions, not so that you control the outcome, but in order then to move to what I think is contemplative about this—how is asking this question at this moment with this group opening up something that is beyond this group?"

For Jerry May, "the crucial question is: *How do you participate in whatever God's up to in that congregation's spiritual life?*"

I'll end with Tilden Edwards's comments on the role of spiritual companion:

I have a sense that this person can "symbolize" to people a lot more than appears on the surface. Their presence and purpose is an incarnate way of showing the congregation that the Spirit really is alive in their midst, "and so let's look at that together." The presence of this person is not just presence in the past, or talking about it in the present, but a presence that becomes an opening in the moment revealing, through this new kind of congregational intervention, something of what is embodied and real right there in the moment. This revelatory moment becomes a point of deepening conversion, corporately and individually. So the value of the spiritual companion's presence, like that of an individual's spiritual director or the priest of a parish, can outweigh anything that they might actually do in the church. This says to me that the personal belief of the Spirit's presence in our midst moment by moment, and how the person expresses this, becomes perhaps the foundational qualification of the companion. In a sense they are a special kind of evangelist holding up the good news of the intimate presence of the Spirit in the congregation's life, and helping people to identify and follow that Presence.

I believe we are describing a very pioneering kind of new way of being an interventionist in the congregational setting and in a way a spiritual teacher. Even though you say, "I'm not here to teach," in a way you do teach just by your way of being present.

EVALUATING THE ROLE

Here are some evaluation comments that seem to touch, in part, on the usefulness of this role, within the total context of the project:

a. Do you feel your church has deepened its spirituality in the last two years? In what way?

MARY SULERUD: Yes, we've been given a rare opportunity to reflect on the nature of our spiritual life, give voice to what it is, shape how it defines us. It is an essential part of a congregation's identity and yet seldom discussed per se. So this project has planted seeds of discussion, prayer and presence of the Spirit we'll be seeing for years.

STEVE HAYWARD: Several of those involved in the work have found a deeper meaning in their faith and the worship life of the church. We have instituted regular evening prayer worship and an additional [contemporary] worship service as a result of looking at the needs of our community. There has not been a general enlightenment within the parish on spiritual matters, but it is something we will continue to work on through regular prayer and an opening-up in faith language in parish life . . . . Our individual conversations helped give me focus on the possibilities and prevented me from getting too overwhelmed.

b. What role do you think your participation in the Congregational Spirituality Project has had in that development?

MARY SULERUD: It has put the idea of congregational spirituality on the "front burner." Which means, amid all the other congregational development tasks, the spiritual development of the congregation beyond preaching, worship on Sundays and weekdays, the usual prayer [and] Bible Study groups, has to be examined, understood, and given space and tools to deepen.

STEVE HAYWARD: Primarily as a motivator. We were stumbling along, looking for a way to get started. Our conversations gave us a boost and a forum for getting the discussion going.

WHERE MIGHT YOUR CHURCH GO FROM HERE?

Now let's consider various ways these learnings about the role of spiritual companion might be relevant to you in uncovering your church's hidden spirit.

There may be benefits to your church from teaming up with an outside spiritual companion for the process of uncovering your church's hidden spirituality. There is always an advantage to having someone come from outside with the freedom to ask the questions that aren't asked anymore and notice the significant surprises that no longer surprise your long-term members.

If your church would like to work with a spiritual companion, you may find that you already know somebody: possibly a person in the judicatory office or a retired judicatory executive who is spiritually attuned, or a trained spiritual guide who has some knowledge of and experience of congregations.[5] If a possible companion comes to mind, you might ask them to look over this book and consider walking alongside you. If you can't think of anybody to ask, you might listen to Henri Nouwen's advice: "The first and nearly spontaneous reaction to the idea of a spiritual guide is, 'Spiritual guides are hard to find.' This might be true, but at least part of the reason for this lack of spiritual guides is that we ourselves do not appeal to our fellow human beings in such a way as to invite them to become our spiritual leaders."[6]

Chuck Olsen, who has worked with many kinds of church groups seeking ways to be more discerning, describes a flurry of experiments. Many multiple-staff churches are changing the role of the director of Christian education to "director of Christian formation" and finding many ways for such a staff person to serve as a spiritual director for the meetings of the congregation. One member of a judicatory staff works with the development of parish councils and puts together discernment leadership teams in each parish. Various internal consultants (as distinguished from those who come from outside the church) are being trained in discernment. I have the sense of a yeasty time in congregations, as they increasingly seek ways of deepening their spiritual lives.

Another way you might get the benefit of the perceptions of people outside the congregation would be to team up with another church. Find a nearby parish with similar interests in spiritual development. You might surface the lay spiritual leaders of the congregation by using the questionnaire in chapter 10. You could design a training session on interviewing (perhaps using the section "The Process of the Interview") and then let each one interview someone in the other church—teaming up to listen for the church's gifts. You might explore deepening the role of the role of the lay spiritual leaders as an ongoing discernment group meeting with the pastor.

You may end up deciding that this discernment is something your church needs to undertake without any external assistance. In that case, your discernment group might make use of the suggestions in the note on page 106 about journal writing prayerfully in response to the interview questions, and sharing your responses with one another. Clergy may also wish to consider new lights on the pastor's role, such as those presented by Howard Friend and Eugene Peterson. Probably, as you read about the role of spiritual companion, you responded, "I do some of that!" Friend writes about the time when "A new way of being a leader began to become clear. I think of this new way as *simply being present*.[7] It is nothing dramatic. Indeed, that is just the point. It is a matter of simply and quietly 'being there.' Since that day, I have paddled less. I navigate less. I overwork and overgive less. And paradoxically, my leadership seems to have become more effective and more empowering."[8]

Eugene Peterson experienced a similar shift: "The paradigm shift that I am after is from pastor as program director to pastor as spiritual director . . . .In program direction, the pastor is Ptolomaic—at the center. In spiritual direction, the pastor is Copernican—in orbit to [or around] the center. . . . At some point along the way I cross a line—my messianic work takes center stage and Messiah is pushed to the sidelines."[9] You might also turn to the work of John Ackerman, who, in his *Spiritual Awakening: A Guide to Spiritual Life in Congregations*, describes many ways a pastor can deepen parish spiritual life.

REVIEWING OUR PATH

At a time when people inside and outside churches are crying out for help with their spiritual search, we need to find ways to respond to that cry within the life of the local congregation. This research is intended as one of those ways, and the five congregations are our pathfinders.

Throughout this exploration, we have tried to take God-at-work in the churches seriously. From that foundation we began with the question "What is congregational spirituality?" and looked for hints in the stories of churches. We often found those hints hidden in hard times in the churches' lives. Telling the story one more time at St. Thomas', Hal concluded, "The fire cleansed us. . . . The people who stayed, stayed for reasons other than buildings and prestige and social status, because there was no building, there was no prestige, and there was no social status. . . . The residual people were committed to some basic things." It was as though a rock crashed into the stream of congregational life, and then the stream found a way to flow on into a new future. Churches like St. Thomas' understood their lives in the pattern of death and resurrection, and in retelling their story they knew it as a holy story.

They also saw their holy story in the power of the discovery that differences of sexual orientation and race commonly resulting in hurtful separation were transformed into a deep "knowing of ourselves as one communion"—an experience members described as "coming from love," adding to "the beauty of life," "a moving spiritual thing," seeing in other faces "the face of God." And this experience birthed a call to this part of the Body of Christ: *Be who you are*, because our society, where people have to work together, to "accept leadership from all kinds of folks," needs an example of "how this can work."

We can see this example not only in the communion of parish life, but also in the lives of the parishioners who walk out the doors empowered by the transforming Spirit they sensed at the altar, and return to the places where they need to be in the midst of the world. If they are transformed people, they can be trusted to go out, "each a seed scattered by the Spirit of God," and minister in the workplace, neighborhood, and families that only they can really know.

So this and the other stories illustrated some of the ways congregations begin to discover, and act out of an awareness of, their hidden spirits as they celebrate the discovery of new life in telling "our story," as it shines through the transparent liturgy, and as they find ways to be incarnate as the church in this place.

How might we, too, uncover the hidden spirit in our own congregation? We might find some hints in the discernment stories of the churches, as they met to ask, "How are we together being grounded in God?" and "What are the special gifts of this community of God's people?" Steve remembered that the people of St. Peter's were "stumbling along, looking for a way to get started, to begin to realize how our busyness has allowed us to avoid the contemplative grounding of our life together." Then the process of their discernment meeting announced: "Stay open to surprises!" As we sought wholeness, we looked at ways of being whole in our way of seeking.

We then looked at some ways of participating in whatever God is up to in our congregation's life—discovering the lay spiritual leaders (the "sages" in our midst) and listening to their wisdom. And we found some ways to reflect theologically on stories from our corporate life. We considered prayer as background and foreground of our journey, questions of timing, and various ways of finding helpers for the discernment process.

And all along we tried to ground the study in faith, a faith that God shares divine life with the churches, and that any attempt to understand the life of the churches is, ultimately, an attempt to know God more truly. And yet, it's more than "understanding"; what prompts the vitality and the growth is the process that we go through together toward that end. Our search is concerned not just with "doing church right": we're hoping to move into ever-deepening relationship with one another in our congregation and with God, attending to those relationships as they grow and evolve, until they are completed in God's grace, in God's own self.

And so we pray to begin and end our quest in the One "who by the power at work within us is able to accomplish abundantly far more than all we can ask or imagine" (Eph. 3:20).

We Want to Learn from You!

Help all of us learn more. You will be able to do more than we could do in a two-year action-research process with just five churches. I invite you to become a valued part of this research enterprise, to help us carry it forward by sharing your learnings, which I will undertake to gather and make available to you and others.

SOME SUGGESTED QUESTIONS

1. Describe what you have discovered about your church's hidden spirit.
2. What ways of uncovering communal gifts and discerning call were most useful to you?
3. Based on your discernment, how is your congregation gifted?
4. Out of your discernment, what sense of shared call has emerged (expressed in being and/or doing)?
5. What ways did you discover for broadening participation in the discernment, drawing more of the congregation into being a part of it?
6. What is the next step right before you now?
7. Out of your story, what are the vital discoveries you would share with a friend in another church? What has been shown you about what's most important in the discernment process?

Send your story to Celia Hahn (cahahn@erols.com) or mail to Celia Hahn, c/o The Alban Institute, Inc., 7315 Wisconsin Avenue, Suite 1250W, Bethesda, MD 20814-3211, by December 31, 2002.

Congregational Spirituality Research: Evaluation Plan

The evaluation process may not only interest research-minded readers, but may also suggest some ideas to parish discernment groups for evaluating their work.

1. Purpose of evaluation:
   a. To provide an occasion for rectors and other participants to reflect on these two years, notice (and therefore reinforce) learnings, and think about next steps that are important to them
   b. To help me learn what has been helpful to rectors, what unhelpful, and what rectors have learned
   c. To provide an opportunity for lay interviewees to reflect on their experience and to teach me about what was helpful and unhelpful
   d. To evaluate the project with research advisors
2. Method of evaluation
   a. Written evaluation forms for clergy, lay interviewees, and research advisors
   b. Conversation with rectors following written exercise (suggest they "pray over it")
3. Purpose of research as stated in original proposal:
   a. To find ways to support and enhance the spiritual development of parishes
   b. To find ways to help parishes discern their gifts and call
   c. To encourage a spirituality that strengthens members to move out into their ministries in the world
4. New purposes that emerged in the course of the research:
   a. To discover the nature of congregational spirituality and some of its most important expressions

    b. To learn how to be a faithful and appropriately helpful spiritual companion to a congregation

5. Questions for rectors:

    a. Do you feel that your church has deepened its spirituality in the last two years? In what way?

    b. What role do you think your participation in the Congregational Spirituality Project has had in that development?

    c. What have been the most important learnings for you in the project?

    d. What parts of the project do you feel have been most helpful? Least helpful? Why and how? For instance:

        i.   Interviews

        ii. Our individual conversations

        iii. Resources provided

        iv. Clarification of gifts

        v.   Discernment process

        vi. Reports from research advisory committee meetings

        vii. Other

    e. Can you see any effect that the experience has had on the interviewees?

        i.   The interview experience?

        ii. Being surfaced as a lay spiritual leader?

        iii. Any other effects?

    f. Based on your experience, what advice would you give other congregations seeking to deepen their spiritual lives? Are there other resources you would recommend?

    g. Was there anything in this experience that surprised you? Describe.

    h. What next steps seem to you to be important in the growth of your congregation's spirituality?

        i.   Is there a step you feel it is very important to take soon? Why? When and how might you plan to take that step?

6. Questions to ask interviewees.

    a. What has it meant to you:

        i.   to be chosen as an interviewee?

        ii. to be interviewed?

        iii. to continue as part of this research (including any meetings you have attended)?

    b. What parts of the experience were positive for you? In what way?

    c. What parts of the experience were negative for you? In what way?

d. What difference do you think it has made to your parish to be part of this research?
e. Was there anything in this experience that surprised you? Describe.
7. Questions for the research advisory committee:
    a. Do you have any summary reflections at this time on
        i.   Learnings about congregational spirituality?
        ii. This project, looking back on your participation and experience?
        iii. The emerging role of spiritual companion?
    b. Are there any other evaluative comments you'd like to add at this time?

Preface

1. *Trinity News*, Trinity Church, 74 Trinity Place, New York, NY 10006.

2. Charles Olsen, *Transforming Church Boards into Communities of Spiritual Leaders* (Bethesda: Alban Institute, 1995).

3. Steve Jacobsen, *Hearts to God, Hands to Work: Connecting Spirituality and Work* (Bethesda: Alban Institute, 1997).

4. Interviewees are referred to by their real names or by pseudonyms, according to their preferences.

Prologue

1. Corinne Ware, *Discover Your Spiritual Type* (Bethesda: Alban Institute, 1995).

2. Christopher D. Ringwald, "Meatless Fridays: Recovering the Virtues of Tradition," *Washington Post*, Dec. 7, 1997, C3.

3. Henri J. M. Nouwen, *Reaching Out: The Three Movements of the Spiritual Life* (New York: Image Books [Doubleday], 1975, 1986), 151-52.

Chapter 1

1. From the hymn "How Firm a Foundation, Ye Saints of the Lord," usually attributed to "K. in John Rippon's Selection, 1787," and found in most current mainline church hymnals.

2. Gerald May, *Care of Mind/Care of Spirit* (San Francisco: Harper & Row, 1982), 61.

3. *Lift Every Voice and Sing II: An African American Hymnal* [Episcopal] (New York: Church Hymnal Corp., 1993).

4. Jacques Pasquier, "Experiences of Conversion," *The Way*, vol. 17, no. 2, April 1977, 115.

Chapter 2

1. Thomas Merton, *The Genesee Diary* (New York: Image Books [Doubleday], 1989), 36.

2. Robert Wuthnow, *After Heaven: Spirituality in America Since the 1950s* (Berkeley and Los Angeles: University of California Press, 1998).

3. Dorothy C. Bass and Craig Dykstra, "Christian Practices and Congregational Education in Faith," in Michael Warren, ed., *The Local Church and the Structures of Change* (Portland, Ore.: Pastoral Press, 2000).

Chapter 3

1. *Lift Every Voice and Sing II.*

2. Nouwen, *Reaching Out,* 154.

Chapter 4

1. Thomas Merton, as quoted in Tilden Edwards, *Spiritual Friend: Reclaiming the Gift of Spiritual Direction* (New York: Paulist Press, 1980), 88.

2. Bruce Reed, *The Dynamics of Religion* (London: Darton, Longman & Todd, 1978).

3. Edwards, *Spiritual Friend,* 80

Chapter 5

1. Reed, *Dynamics of Religion,* 157ff.

2. Metropolitan John Zizioulas, "The Church as Communion," *St. Vladimir's Theological Quarterly,* 1994.

Part II Prologue

1. This summary owes much to wisdom offered to a group of spiritual leaders by some thoughtful contemplatives—Rose Mary Dougherty, Gerald May, and Tilden Edwards, all of the Shalem Institute for Spiritual Formation.

2. Charles Olsen can help us with part of this task. He has developed faithful means for church boards to do their work and has described these in his books: *Transforming Church Boards into Communities of Spiritual Leaders* (Bethesda: Alban Institute, 1995) and *Discovering God's Will Together* (Bethesda: Alban Institute; and Nashville: Upper Room, 1997). And Suzanne Farnham and her coauthors, Stephanie A. Hall and R. Taylor

McLean, provide specific suggestions for reorienting church meetings toward discernment and prayerfulness in *Grounded in God: Listening Hearts Discernment for Group Deliberations* (Harrisburg, Pa.: Morehouse, 1999).

3. Gerald May, "Contemplative Spiritual Formation: An Introduction," privately circulated article, Shalem Institute for Spiritual Formation, Dec. 1994.

4. Howard E. Friend, Jr., *Recovering the Sacred Center: Church Renewal from the Inside Out* (Valley Forge: Judson, 1998), 7.

5. Friend, *Recovering the Sacred Center*, 9.

6. T. S. Eliot, "Four Quartets," as quoted in David Steindl-Rast, *A Listening Heart: The Spirituality of Sacred Sensuousness* (New York: Crossroad, 1983, 1999), 99.

7. Wuthnow, *After Heaven*, 191.

8. Walter Brueggemann, "Gathering the Church in the Spirit: Reflections on Exile and the Inscrutable Mind of God," a pamphlet (Decatur, Ga.: CTS Press, 1995).

9. Wuthnow, *After Heaven*, 191.

10. Gerald G. May, Will and Spirit (San Francisco: HarperSanFrancisco, 1982), 163.

11. Friend, *Recovering the Sacred Center*, 104.

12. Farnham et al., *Grounded in God*, as quoted in Gilbert Rendle, Leading Change in the Congregation, 9.

Chapter 6

1. Here again I am grateful to Howard Friend's work.

2. An informal method of Bible study that has migrated to this country from Africa. The version I have (a mimeographed sheet) is headed "An African Method for Bible Study" with a note, "The source is Mumpko Theological Institute of South Africa."

Chapter 7

1. Walter Wink, *Transforming Bible Study* (Nashville: Abingdon, 1980).

2. A few quotes from these pages are included in the following design and are indicated by quotation marks.

3. Wink, *Transforming Bible Study*.

4. Wink, *Transforming Bible Study*.

5. Wink, *Transforming Bible Study*.

6. Wink, *Transforming Bible Study*.

7. Wink, *Transforming Bible Study*.
8. Wink, *Transforming Bible Study*.
9. Wink, *Transforming Bible Study*.
10. Wink, *Transforming Bible Study*.

Chapter 8
1. Carolyn Gratton, *The Art of Spiritual Guidance* (New York: Crossroad, 1995), 128.

Chapter 9
1. Edwards, *Spiritual Friend*, 88.

Chapter 11
1. Corinne Ware, *Discover Your Spiritual Type* (Bethesda: Alban Institute, 1995).

Chapter 12
1. Nouwen, *Reaching Out*, 97.
2. Nouwen, *Reaching Out*, 95.
3. Nouwen, *Reaching Out*, 95-96.
4. Nouwen, *Reaching Out*, 95-96.

Chapter 15
1. Denise Woods, *Congregations: The Alban Journal*, Jan.-Feb., 1997.
2. Thomas Hart, *The Art of Christian Listening* (Mahwah, N.J.: Paulist, 1980), 8.
3. Margaret Guenther, *Holy Listening: The Art of Spiritual Direction* (Cambridge, Mass.: Cowley Press, 1992), 92-93.
4. Corinne Ware, *Connecting to God: Nurturing Spirituality through Small Groups* (Bethesda: Alban Institute, 1997), 7.
5. For trained spiritual guides, you might get in touch with the Shalem Institute for Spiritual Formation, which has graduates in many parts of the country. Call (301) 897-7334. As part of the third year of the project, I am working to test and explore the role of spiritual companion congregations. As of fall 2000, we had a group of five trained, experienced companions who discern this work as their calling and are meeting with churches in the Washington, D.C., area.
6. Nouwen, *Reaching Out*, 137.

7. Italics added.

8. Friend, *Recovering the Sacred Center*, 149.

9. Eugene Peterson, *Under the Unpredictable Plant: An Exploration in Vocational Holiness* (Grand Rapids: Eerdmans, 1992), 175-76, 179.

Ackerman, John. *Spiritual Awakening: A Guide to Spiritual Life in Congregations*. Bethesda: Alban Institute, 1994.

Bass, Dorothy C., ed. *Practicing Our Faith: A Way of Life for a Searching People*. San Francisco: Jossey-Bass, 1997.

Bennison, Charles E., Jr., with Kortright Davis, Adair Lummis, and Paula Nesbitt. *In Praise of Congregations*. Cambridge, Mass.: Cowley Publications, 1999.

Brueggemann, Walter. "Gathering the Church in the Spirit: Reflections on Exile and the Inscrutable Wind of God." (pamphlet). Decatur, Ga.: CTS Press, 1955. (Address: P.O. Box 520, Decatur, GA 30031.)

Congregations: The Alban Journal. Jan.-Feb., 1997.

Edwards, Tilden. *Spiritual Friend: Reclaiming the Gift of Spiritual Direction*. New York: Paulist Press, 1980.

Farnham, Suzanne G., Stephanie A. Hull, and R. Taylor McLean. *Grounded in God: Listening Hearts Discernment for Group Deliberations*. Harrisburg, Pa.: Morehouse, 1999.

Friend, Howard E., Jr.. *Recovering the Sacred Center: Church Renewal From the Inside Out*. Valley Forge: Judson, 1998.

Gratton, Carolyn. *The Art of Spiritual Guidance*. New York: Crossroad, 1995.

Guenther, Margaret. *Holy Listening: The Art of Spiritual Direction*. Cambridge, Mass., Cowley Press, 1992.

Hahn, Celia Allison. *Growing in Authority, Relinquishing Control: A New Approach to Faithful Leadership*. Bethesda: Alban Institute, 1994.

Hart, Thomas. *The Art of Christian Listening*. Ramsey, N.J.: Paulist Press, 1980.

The Hymnal 1982 (Episcopal). New York: Church Publishing Inc., 1982.

Johnson, Luke Timothy. *Living Jesus: Learning the Heart of the Gospel.* San Francisco: HarperSanFrancisco, 1999.
Lift Every Voice and Sing II: An African American Hymnal (Episcopal). New York: Church Hymnal Corp., 1993.
May, Gerald G. *Care of Mind/Care Of Spirit.* San Francisco: Harper & Row, 1982.
———. *Will and Spirit.* San Francisco: HarperSanFrancisco, 1982.
Nouwen, Henri J. M. *Reaching Out: The Three Movements of the Spiritual Life.* New York: Image Books (Doubleday), 1975, 1986.
———. *The Genesee Diary.* New York: Image Books (Doubleday), 1981.
Olsen, Charles. *Transforming Church Boards into Communities of Spiritual Leaders.* Bethesda: Alban Institute, 1995.
Oswald, Roy M., and Robert E. Friedrich, Jr. *Discerning Your Congregation's Future: A Strategic and Spiritual Approach.* Bethesda: Alban Institute, 1996.
Pasquier, Jacques. "Experience of Conversion." *The Way,* vol. 17, no. 2, April 1977.
Peterson, Eugene. *Under the Unpredictable Plant: An Exploration in Vocational Holiness.* Grand Rapids: Eerdmans, 1992.
Reed, Bruce. *The Dynamics of Religion: Process and Movement in Christian Churches.* London: Darton, Longman & Todd, 1978.
Schmemann, Alexander. *For the Life of the World: Sacraments and Orthodoxy.* Crestwood, N.Y.: St. Vladimir's Seminary Press, 1973.
Steindl-Rast, David. *A Listening Heart: The Spirituality of Sacred Sensuousness.* New York: Crossroad, 1983, 1999.
———. "The Mystical Core of Organized Religion." *ReVision,* vol. 12, no. 1, summer 1989.
Ware, Corinne. *Connecting to God: Nurturing Spirituality through Small Groups.* Bethesda: Alban Institute, 1997.
———. *Discover Your Spiritual Type.* Bethesda: Alban Institute, 1995.
Wink, Walter. *Transforming Bible Study.* Nashville: Abingdon, 1980.
Wuthnow, Robert. *After Heaven: Spirituality in America Since the 1950s.* Berkeley and Los Angeles: University of California Press, 1998.
Zizioulas, Metropolitan John, "Communion and Otherness." *St. Vladimir's Theological Quarterly.* Crestwood, N.Y.: St. Vladimir's Orthodox Theological Seminary, 1994.
———. "The Church as Communion" *St. Vladimir's Theological Quarterly.* Crestwood, N.Y.: St. Vladimir's Orthodox Theological Seminary, 1994.

Welcome to the work of Alban Institute...
the leading publisher and congregational
resource organization for clergy and laity today.

Your purchase of this book means you have an interest in the kinds of information, research, consulting, networking opportunities and educational seminars that Alban Institute produces and provides. Founded in 1974, we are a non-denominational, non-profit membership organization dedicated to providing practical and useful support to religious congregations and those who participate in and lead them.

Alban is acknowledged as a pioneer in learning and teaching on *Conflict Management *Faith and Money *Congregational Growth and Change *Leadership Development *Mission and Planning *Clergy Recruitment and Training *Clergy Support, Self-Care and Transition *Spirituality and Faith Development *Congregational Security.

Our membership is comprised of over 8,000 clergy, lay leaders, congregations and institutions who benefit from:

- ❖ 15% discount on hundreds of Alban books
- ❖ $50 per-course tuition discount on education seminars
- ❖ Subscription to *Congregations*, the Alban journal (a $30 value)
- ❖ Access to Alban research and (soon) the "Members-Only" archival section of our web site www.alban.org

For more information on Alban membership, books, consulting, and leadership enrichment seminars, visit our Web Site: **www.alban.org** or call **1-800-486-1318, ext.243.**

The Alban Institute
Bethesda, MD